BUILDING LOVE TOGETHER IN BLENDED FAMILIES

The 5 Love Languages® and Becoming Stepfamily Smart

GARY CHAPMAN, PhD
and RON L. DEAL, MMFT

NORTHFIELD PUBLISHING | CHICAGO

Published in association with the literary agency of MacGregor Literary, Inc.

Edited by Elizabeth Cody Newenhuyse
Interior and cover design: Erik M. Peterson
Gary Chapman photo: P.S. Photography
Ron Deal photo: Amy Bell

Library of Congress Cataloging-in-Publication Data
Names: Chapman, Gary D., 1938- author. | Deal, Ron L., author.
Title: Building love together in blended families : the 5 love languages
   and becoming stepfamily smart / Gary Chapman and Ron L. Deal.
Description: Chicago : Northfield Publishing, [2020] | Includes
   bibliographical references. | Summary: "Learn how to create a loving and
   safe environment amidst the unique challenges of a blended family in
   this new book from Ron Deal and bestselling author of The 5 Love
   Languages®, Gary Chapman"-- Provided by publisher.
Identifiers: LCCN 2019036525 (print) | LCCN 2019036526 (ebook) | ISBN
   9780802419057 (paperback) | ISBN 9780802497734 (ebook)
Subjects: LCSH: Stepfamilies. | Communication in families. | Love.
Classification: LCC HQ759.92 .C48 2020 (print) | LCC HQ759.92 (ebook) |
   DDC 306.874/7--dc23
LC record available at https://lccn.loc.gov/2019036525
LC ebook record available at https://lccn.loc.gov/2019036526

We hope you enjoy this book from Northfield Publishing. Our goal is to provide high-quality, thought-provoking books and products that connect truth to your real needs and challenges. For more information on other books and products that will help you with all your important relationships, go to northfieldpublishing.com or write to:

Northfield Publishing
820 N. LaSalle Boulevard
Chicago, IL 60610

1 3 5 7 9 10 8 6 4 2

Printed in the United States of America

Praise for *Building Love Together in Blended Families*

In this accessible and game-changing guide, Dr. Gary Chapman and Ron Deal delve into the real issues stepfamilies face but often don't know how to talk about. With a unique approach based on The 5 Love Languages model, they provide a practical and empowering path forward for parents and children alike.

LORI GOTTLIEB | *New York Times* bestselling author of *Maybe You Should Talk to Someone*

The complex emotional challenges often associated with stepfamilies have proven challenging for countless people—and the fallout can be incredibly painful. However, Gary Chapman and Ron Deal have good news: it's more than possible for blended families to enjoy thriving relationships! Their new book brings together their combined and time-tested wisdom to show you how your own blended family can flourish amidst your "new normal."

JIM DALY | President, Focus on the Family

What an incredible resource! Nobody but Gary and Ron, two world-class experts, could have written this powerful book. The wisdom they impart is priceless. Every couple in a blended family—and every extended family member connected to them—needs to read this valuable book. It's engaging, grounded and immeasurably practical.

LES AND LESLIE PARROTT | #1 *New York Times* bestselling authors of *Saving Your Marriage Before It Starts*

The blended family is a new norm in our culture and world. It involves so many difficult challenges and complexities in the search for ways to promote healthy parenting, love, safety, healing, and structure. Gary Chapman and Ron Deal have written the best book I have read on the subject. They are clear, straightforward, and practical in the steps and skills they provide, especially in how the five love languages apply to the relationships. Chapter 1 alone is worth the price of the book. Highly recommended.

JOHN TOWNSEND | *New York Times* bestselling author of the Boundaries book series
Founder, the Townsend Institute for Leadership and Counseling

I cannot think of a better layer to add to the blended family conversation than the understanding of how each of us view the world. We all have a different lens with which we see the world—our circumstances and situations. We each have our own "language" that is uniquely ours or uniquely theirs. As we begin to understand one another's language, we can better understand how to recognize and meet each other's needs. From parents to children. I cannot think of a more dynamic duo in this blended conversation than Ron Deal and Gary Chapman.

SANDI PATTY PESLIS | Artist and mom to a beautiful blended family

To the thousands of families I've worked with who didn't feel so much blended as busted? This. This is the book we've all been waiting for. Gary Chapman and Ron Deal have cracked the code for those of us who are living with other people's children and are longing to love them with honesty and compassion. Not only will the words within these pages strengthen your family, they will ground your marriage in new and deeper ways. This book is essential reading for any stepparent.

KATHI LIPP | Bestselling author of *The Husband Project* and coauthor of *But I'm Not a Wicked Stepmom*

So often two families are put together without being prepared for the challenges ahead, *Building Love Together in Blended Families* is a great tool for preparing everyone involved. It allows you to reach for the others in the family that is to be. To love the way another most powerfully feels loved is the foundation of a blended family.

STEPHEN ARTERBURN | Author and Founder of New Life LIVE!

Creating a loving home is why couples form a blended family. But the process takes time and purpose. As a social researcher, I've seen that all parties—parents, stepparents, the children themselves—long for great relationships. I've also seen that understanding each other is the missing link. I can't think of two experts better suited to help you do that than Ron Deal and Gary Chapman. This is a fantastic book, and is the essential guide all blended families need.

SHAUNTI FELDHAHN | Social researcher and bestselling author of *For Women Only, For Parents Only*, and *The Kindness Challenge*

Ron Deal and Gary Chapman are absolutely the perfect blend to enrich your blended family relationships. With over three decades of experience, Ron is THE leading authority globally on blended families. None better. And Gary, he is one of the top writers of our day. This is destined to be a bestseller and a classic for blended families everywhere.

DENNIS RAINEY | Cofounder, FamilyLife

In our work with married couples, we've found that many of the most complicated issues facing modern marriages stem from blended family dynamics. In this powerful and practical new book, Gary Chapman and Ron Deal draw on their unparalleled expertise to masterfully unravel the complexities of blended family dynamics. Every chapter felt like a master class for spouses, parents and stepparents. This book will be a game-changer for every blended family!

DAVE AND ASHLEY WILLIS | Authors of *The Naked Marriage* and hosts of *The Naked Marriage* podcast

When you love someone, you can't help but show and tell about the people you love. But the realities of life and complexities of blended families can take their toll in living it out. This book, by two highly regarded relationship experts, will help you love your family more completely and with greater wisdom than ever before. You'll love it and grow because of it, too!

DAVID ROBBINS | President and CEO of FamilyLife

When I think of the most outstanding authority on marriage I know, I think of Gary Chapman and when I think of my go-to person on blended families, I think of Ron Deal. This book is a combination of the best of both of these two incredible writers and communicators. I loved every page in this most helpful book.

JIM BURNS | President, HomeWord; author, *Doing Life with Your Adult Children*

Stepfamilies and first families are inherently different. The same rules just don't apply. Adapting *The 5 Love Languages* to fit blended family life? Brilliant! This is the book every remarried couple needs to read—together!

BRENDA OCKUN | Founder and publisher, *StepMom Magazine*

Step families need a common language to build trust, connection, and new attachments. *Building Love Together in Blended Families* provides a path to "speak love" mutually so each family member can accept the love they need to grow closer. This is a wonderful hands-on resource.

GIL AND BRENDA STUART | Authors of *Restored and Remarried*

This book offers valuable insight on how to apply the well-known principles of the five love languages in blended family relationships with those who may—or may not—seek to receive love or offer love in return. It's practical, realistic, and inspiring. If you're in a blended family, you need this book.

GAYLA GRACE | Author of *Stepparenting with Grace: A Devotional for Blended Families*

The 5 Love Languages has had such a major impact on our marriage and *The Smart Stepfamily* gave us a roadmap to navigate blended family life. But Ron Deal and Gary Chapman's collaboration in *Building Love Together in Blended Families* really gave us a blueprint for building long, lasting, loving relationships in our home.

LAMAR AND RONNIE TYLER | Speakers and cofounders of BlackandMarriedwithKids.com

From Gary:
*I dedicate this book to
the many blended families who have
shared their journey with me through the years.*

From Ron:
*To my wife, Nan, for your faithful partnership
as we build and mature our love for each other.
And to the thousands of blended families
who have shared with me your story of
finding and building love together. You inspire me.*

Books by Gary Chapman

The 5 Love Languages
The 5 Love Languages of Children (with Ross Campbell)
The 5 Love Languages of Teenagers
A Teen's Guide to the 5 Love Languages
The DIY Guide to Building a Family That Lasts (with Shannon Warden)
Anger
When Sorry Isn't Enough (with Jennifer Thomas)
The Marriage You've Always Wanted
The Family You've Always Wanted

The Smart Stepfamily Series
Author/coauthor and Consulting Editor Ron L. Deal

The Smart Stepfamily (book, DVD series, and Participant's Guide)
The Smart Stepfamily Marriage (with David H. Olson)
The Smart Stepfamily Guide to Financial Planning (with Greg S. Pettys and David O. Edwards)
The Smart Stepmom (with Laura Petherbridge)
The Smart Stepdad
Daily Encouragement for the Smart Stepfamily (with Dianne Neal Matthews)
Dating and the Single Parent
Life in a Blender (booklet for kids)

Contents

About the Authors   9

Introduction   11

1 Blending Well, Loving Well   15

2 Understanding the Languages of Love   33

3 When Loves Compete and Conflict   65

4 Building Love Together in Your Marriage   83

5 Building Love Together in Stepparenting   97

6 Building Love Together in Sibling Relationships   117

7 Building Love Together in Grandparenting   133

8 Building Love Together in the Face of Rejection   151

9 Encouragement for the Journey Ahead   169

Epilogue   181

Acknowledgments   183

Notes   185

About the Authors

Gary Chapman is the author of the #1 bestselling 5 Love Languages® series and director of Marriage and Family Life Consultants, Inc. He travels the world presenting seminars and has appeared frequently on national media. He and his wife, Karolyn, live in North Carolina. For more information visit 5lovelanguages.com.

Ron L. Deal is one of the most widely read and viewed experts on blended families in the country. He is founder of Smart Stepfamilies™, Director of FamilyLife Blended® for FamilyLife®, the author of numerous videos and books on stepfamily living including the bestselling *The Smart Stepfamily, The Smart Stepmom* (with Laura Petherbridge), *The Smart Stepdad,* and *The Smart Stepfamily Marriage* (with David Olson), and is consulting editor for the Smart Stepfamily Series of books. Ron is a licensed marriage and family therapist, popular conference speaker, host of the podcast *FamilyLife Blended* and a daily one-minute radio feature that airs on more than nine hundred outlets nationwide, and appears regularly on national media. His work has been quoted/referenced by multiple news outlets such as *The New York Times*, *The Wall Street Journal*, and *USA Today*. He and his wife, Nan, have three sons and live in Little Rock, Arkansas. Find events and resources at RonDeal.org.

Introduction

THE FIRST STORY IN the first chapter of my book *The 5 Love Languages* shares the struggles of a man I happened to sit next to on a plane. He had been married three times. Two attempts at "blending" families had failed. "I can't believe it happened to me three times," he said to me, and went on to ask the question so many ask: How does love stay alive in some marriages? How do some make it work?

I do not have to tell you that blended families face their own unique challenges in "making it work." That's why I have teamed with Ron Deal on this new book. We know that you, like my friend on the plane, want to build lasting love in your blended family. But how? How do you *find* love, *strengthen* it, and *keep* it in a stepfamily?

This book combines the key insights of my five love languages concepts with the wisdom of blended family expert Ron Deal (author of the Smart Stepfamily series of books). You see, the five love languages need to be applied differently in a blended family setting. In biological families, the five love languages teach people who are naturally and equally motivated toward loving one another how to love best. As you may have figured out, it isn't always like that in a blended family. We'll teach you how to apply the principles to love people who may or may not care to receive your best love or love you in return. We call that "combining with wisdom."

"But Gary, I already know what the five love languages are." That's great, and you've probably already made some good applications to your family. But you, also, might be like the 70 percent of respondents to one survey who said they had questions or were confused about how to apply the Love Languages specifically to a blended family.[1] Given the different internal dynamics of blended families, being familiar with the Love Language principles is a good start, but insight into how to apply them to a blended family is needed. Survey respondents shared their confusion:

> *"If my stepchild's love language is Quality Time, how do you do that when they don't want to spend time with you?"*

> *"How do you avoid a rivalry between stepsiblings? My stepson's primary love language is Gifts. If I give him a gift and my child sees it, even though their love language isn't gift giving, they still saw the other child receive something they didn't. Does that add to the rivalry between them?"*

> *"Stepparents are pretty sensitive to the needs of their stepkids—I try to love them well—but how do you get the children to be sensitive to the needs of the stepparent?"*

In this book we'll answer these questions and more. So whether your children are young or adults, whether your relationship was preceded by a partner breakup or death, or whether you're considering marriage, just getting started, or already many years down the road, we're glad you've picked up a copy of this book. And if you're a grandparent or extended family member, we appreciate you seeking to offer support. Now, let's build lasting love.

—GARY CHAPMAN

1

Blending Well, Loving Well

WITHOUT BEING TOO presumptuous, we think we know why you bought this book. You want a good blend. No, we're not talking about smoothies or coffee. You want your home to be a healthy place for everyone involved, a good blend of closeness, autonomy, and permanence, knowing you will be there for each other; a good blend of happiness and joy, trust and emotional safety; a good blend of parenting that offers limits, nurturance, and healthy boundaries that teach respect and decency to children so they can grow to be mature and responsible adults who contribute to the world and care for others. Simply put, you want to blend well and love well. A loving, blended family is why you got together (or are starting to date) and that's why you bought this book. Are we right—or pretty close?

"WE KEEP FALLING INTO A HOLE"

A good blend is what Kate[1] wanted, too.

Kate is the mother of three children and stepmother to two. She and her husband, Chris, had been married three years when she reached out for help. "We're making progress," she said, "but we keep falling into a hole." Her three kids, a boy sixteen, a girl thirteen, and a girl nine, lived with them full-time, while his two girls, ages seventeen and eight, kept a traditional every-other weekend visitation schedule with their mom. "My thirteen-year-old, Kayla, is a little sassy," Kate explained. "I try to keep her in line, but she grumbles and complains a lot. I've learned to work around it and make her follow through, but my husband feels disrespected and believes there shouldn't be any back talk and that we should punish her every time. This has been an issue for a while, and now it seems to come up at every turn, even when it's not about Kayla—if one of his kids gets out of line and I try to say something, he defends them, saying, 'Why would you get on mine when you won't get on yours?'" Sometimes stepfamily living is challenging because of multiple intertwined dynamics like this.

We believe the wise application of the five love languages and a good understanding of healthy stepfamilies can help you overcome these challenges. Kate's story reveals some common not-so-blended family dilemmas: a marriage that is being eroded by parental disunity; relatively benign disagreements that quickly feel like malignant betrayals of trust; biological parents who feel stuck in the middle; loyalty conflicts in children; and a death or divorce loss narrative that ever looms in the background, battling for command of new family relationships.

Chris feels disrespected and is likely worried things will get worse as his stepdaughter gets older. Kate feels frustrated and distraught, caught in the middle between two people she loves and cares for deeply. She has tried to find a win-win solution, but no matter what she does somebody seems unhappy and angry with her. Kayla is argumentative (an annoying behavior no parent wants to see in their child), but what really worries Kate is that the family conflict makes her daughter feel singled out, picked on, and rejected by her stepdad (which isn't good for her developing self-esteem). And both Kate and Chris end up unhappy with their marriage. In all, everyone tells the story of their family a little differently, but they agree they don't feel safe and loved. At this rate this will not result in a good blend.

HOW "LOVE" GETS COMPLICATED IN A BLENDED FAMILY

But why is this happening? They love each other, right? Well, yes, they do . . . to varying degrees. You see, that is part of the problem. In blended families sometimes the definitions of love given by children and adults, and the motivation to deepen love, vary widely.

First, let's consider how different definitions of love complicate loving in a blended family. One way to define love is by examining what we call *love associations,* that is, the relational qualities or behaviors associated with love. A stepchild may *love* their stepparent, but that does not necessarily translate into the same level of respect for their authority as it does with a biological parent. A stepparent may *love* all the children the same, but still find it awkward to hug their stepchild. A parent may *love* their new spouse, but not want to add the spouse's name to the life insurance already set up for their children. Stepsiblings may have a blast together and consider one another family, but not want stepsiblings in the annual Christmas family portrait made with Grandma. And step-

> A stepparent may "love" all the children the same, but still find it awkward to hug their stepchild.

grandparents, who *love* all the grandkids equally, may find themselves more willing to babysit if the biological grandchildren are there. You see, it is the associations of love that help give definition to it and determine how it expresses itself in families—and whether people feel loved.

The problems start when the definitions of love between adults and children collide, like Kate's frustration with her daughter for "not letting her stepdad into her heart," and with her husband for "pushing Kayla out of his."

Stepchildren often have a basic level of respect for stepparents (like they would toward a teacher at school). Problems arise, however, when the parent and/or stepparent demand more than that. Likewise, definitions of love are colliding when a biological parent gets angry at their spouse for not offering the same type of hug to the stepchildren as they do their own children, or when a stepparent withdraws love from stepchildren for not including stepsiblings in the annual Christmas portrait. This is also why the level of conflict in the first year of stepfamily living is a bit shocking to many newlyweds. Before marriage they perceived their children as excited for the wedding and becoming a family, but after the honeymoon they experience kids who are dragging their feet. Sometimes it is true that the couple saw only what they wanted to see (approval from the children for them to marry), but other times the kids really were excited for the wedding. But that doesn't mean their definitions of "becoming a loving family" were the same as the adults. Once real life hits and everyone is living under the same roof, gaps in the definitions of love become apparent.

Insiders and outsiders

Definitions of love also differ among biological family members (what we often refer to as "insiders") and stepfamily members ("outsiders"). Because Kate and Kayla have always been together, Kate understands when to take her daughter's sarcasm as disrespectful. She understands her daughter's moods and when something else is behind her sharp tone. These things are clear to insiders—and more importantly, they don't doubt whether they are loved during their worst moments. Chris, an outsider to all of this, is in a much more fragile place. He is learning to read his stepdaughter's emotional cues, but even when he can look past her outward behavior, he still sees it as disrespect—and with it, the fear that love between the two of them might not develop or mature. Further, if love between them is strained, he is aware that other relationships, like between stepsiblings, will likely be affected.

Clashing definitions of "love" spark hurt, anger, and protest in a family. Some of this is an attempt to push the "offending" person to love in a way more consistent with what the hurt person believes should be happening. But, predictably, this reaction usually backfires in a multitude of ways. (Later we'll show you better ways to respond.) It shames the "unloving" person and tells them they aren't good enough; it makes the hurt person look selfish and immature; it creates conflict and tension in the home; it expands the emotional distance between the persons directly involved. When other family members (like a biological parent) jump in to defend or protect their fellow "insider," additional relationships can become casualties as well.

YOU'RE MOTIVATED TO LOVE, THEY'RE STILL DECIDING

Members of blended families can differ greatly in their *motivation to love* and love deeply. For example, in some stepfamilies only the couple has a need for a good blend while the children are fine if it never happens. This is predictably true the first year or so for stepfamilies with teenagers. It is often the case well be-yond the first year with later-life stepfamilies (sometimes called adult stepfamilies) that are born when the stepchildren are adults. Frequently, adult stepchildren don't have a need to bond with a stepparent, let alone love them. In fact, many adult stepchildren don't even identify themselves as part of a stepfamily or think of their parent's new spouse as their stepparent. We've had multiple conversations with adults whose parent has been remarried for years, and it never occurred to them to view their parent's spouse as anything other than "Dad's wife." This reality is discour-aging to many stepparents who very much want to form a trusting mutual relationship with their stepchildren.

> Chasing a child's approval puts you in a position of weakness.

We'll talk more in detail about this later, but we should briefly mention here that this gap in motivation complicates parenting younger children tremendously. For example, one quality of good parents is they don't worry about winning their kids' approval. You see, chasing a child's approval puts you in a position of weakness. It makes you hesitate when you need to set a boundary. This dy-namic puts stepparents at a distinct disadvantage, especially when it's clear the child is not nearly as motivated toward love as the stepparent.

Complicating all this is the underlying presence of loss in the family. Parents *need* the family to blend—and they *need* their children to *need* it to blend, too. Why? Because parents want to restore for their kids (no matter their age) what was lost to death, divorce, or a breakup. They want their children to be part of a loving family that will nurture and care for them well into the future. In addition, many parents don't want to feel guilty for exposing their children to a fractured family, even if it primarily wasn't their fault. What parents passionately and desperately want is for love to "win the day" in their stepfamily home. And not just surface love; they want a deep, abiding, trusting, leaning-on-each-other type of love.

Well, of course, they—and *you*—do. *Love and loving* is what heals our souls and gives us confidence, identity, passion, a sense of meaning, and the energy to charge into the world. Love is what reveals us, affirms us, values us, forgives us, and redeems us. It connects us to He who first loved us and empowers us to extend God's love to others. *Love and loving* result in a compassionate society that reaches across social, racial, economic, political, and national lines and unifies people. It builds bridges of mercy and grace that traverse territorial divides—whether political or familial—and connects the hearts of people. So, of course, this is what you want and need. Your children, however, just might not share in your need to the same degree.

The question, given varying definitions of love and motivations to love, is how do you accomplish a good blend? How does a blended family best pursue a loving home when there are varying definitions of what love should look like and varying motivations to make it happen? If you're blessed enough to have children who are also motivated toward deepening love, you'll find a good blend easier to achieve. If you're not, the degree of difficulty just went up considerably. Either way, forming a good blend begins by becoming stepfamily smart.

NAVIGATING THE STEPFAMILY OCEAN

The relational structure of a blended family is different than a biological family so you have to get smart about stepfamily living.* For example, the fact that one parent has a bonded, biological relationship with their child(ren) that predates the couple's marriage is a significant difference. This has implications for parent, stepparent, and sibling roles in the home, and affects everything from how people grieve, to finances, to marital trust, to co-parenting with an ex-spouse.

That's why I (Ron) like to say that blended family couples swim in a different ocean than first-marriage couples. The stepfamily ocean has a cooler water temperature (steprelationships tend to have less warmth). Most everyone in a stepfamily has experienced a significant loss that is always just under the surface. This ocean has more sharks (former spouses, co-parenting issues, and the stress of merging to name a few). And the water is less clear (stepfamily life is murky: roles are unclear, rituals and traditions hazy, and relationships lack definition). To navigate this ocean well requires that you understand and follow a few blended family principles for loving well.

BLENDED FAMILY PRINCIPLES FOR LOVING WELL

Principle #1: Blended families are not born with a sense of "familyness"; your journey nurtures it.

Fundamentally, the journey of a blended family is the search for a shared identity. "Who are we to one another?" is the first

---

* Beyond this book we recommend Ron's bestselling book *The Smart Stepfamily: Seven Steps to a Healthy Family*, which is the first book of the Smart Stepfamily Series of books for stepmoms, stepdads, and stepcouples. Learn more at SmartStepfamilies.com and FamilyLife.com/blended.

question everyone is asking. Parents often try to answer it quickly. "There's no 'mine' or 'yours' in this family. We're family now. You're all 'my' kids." But what does that really mean? Is that true with adult children the way it might be with younger children? And does everyone embrace the "we" language or does that feel intrusive in some way?

You have to journey to the "land of us" before you can say, "This is us." The bonds of love have to be nurtured, agreed upon, and valued by all. On day one, blended families are not blended. They are a collection of insiders and outsiders in search of familyness. While pursuing this goal, being patient with the process is critical.

Principle #2: Patience is a virtue. While waiting, love generously.

Because motivations to love vary between adults and children, insiders and outsiders, it is important for family members to relax their expectations for the family. Assuming, as many people do, that children will love their stepsiblings and the stepparent just because the couple has fallen in love and decided to marry is a huge setup. Now, if that happens, sing your praises and keep marching on. But usually there's at least a gap in the timing of when this happens and to what depth bonding takes place. Softening your expectations is not about giving up hope; it is about becoming realistic about the timing and pace of bonding within your home. Learning to be patient is important.

Because the average blended family needs between five and seven years to merge and form a shared family identity,[2] I (Ron) tell couples to create their family with a "slow cooker" approach, not a blender.[3] Blenders have blades! Slow cookers blend ingredients quietly and over a longer period of time. Ingredients are left intact when first put into the pot (we call that moment a wedding) and are allowed to soften and begin to share of themselves in their own timing. This is a critical concept that can dramatically change the outcome of your family journey. When parents, as we alluded to previously, try to force love they violate the integrity of the ingredients. You may be trying to make stew, but smashing the carrots or potatoes isn't helpful or even necessary when using a slow cooker. Ingredients will eventually share what they have to offer entirely on their own and they don't need to be mangled in the process. The trick in the beginning is respecting the firm, sometimes-rigid exterior of ingredients (like carrots) while gently inviting them to soften and join with the others to make something everyone can enjoy. This low-level "heat" is in part what this book will help you do. Loving with wisdom softens the heart. But make no mistake about it, even when you get it right, it still takes many hours to cook something in a slow pot and it often takes years to blend a stepfamily.

So, while you're waiting for ingredients to warm up and soften, then combine with other ingredients, remember to love generously. This doesn't mean throwing yourself indiscriminately onto others or violating their space (we'll talk about pacing with other ingredients in a later chapter). Nor does it mean to overextend yourself to those who are closed toward you. However, it does mean to be generous, persistent, steadfast, and sacrificial with your love, even toward those who aren't generous in return. When waiting on someone else to warm up, most people withdraw to a safe place. But if you "go cold," it's unlikely the other person will become warm. Someone must always go first. Your motivation makes you the best candidate.

Principle #3: A committed, loving marriage is the first and last motivator of stepfamily integration, so strengthen your marriage.

Of course, you want a loving marriage. And one that lasts. Research by Dr. David Olson and me (Ron) reveals that there are unique aspects of forming a strong blended family marriage. In our book *The Smart Stepfamily Marriage* we report that, like all couples, stepcouples must manage the internal aspects of marriage related to things like communication, finances, and resolving conflict. However, what often blindsides couples are the external "sharks" that surround them in the stepfamily ocean. Parenting dilemmas, a difficult ex-spouse, and not knowing how to balance loyalties to children and the new marriage can take bites out of the couple's solidarity.

And while these dynamics are stressful in and of themselves, they add to the fear of another relationship failure or loss. And fear, ironically, makes failure more likely. The insidious truth about fear, our research confirmed, is that if I am concerned that you're not committed to me and/or my children I will become guarded, self-protective, distrustful, and reactive. And when I'm protecting me from you there cannot be an "us."

> Your loving marriage encourages the members of your family to eventually love one another.

Considered together, we believe couples in stepfamilies have more internal and external stressors on their relationship than most couples. Learning to love each other well includes learning to speak your spouse's love language and getting smart about swimming in the stepfamily ocean.

A loving marriage obviously does a lot for you. Beyond that, it also has a huge impact on the motivation of your family members to love one another. Just as the love of a highly motivated person bids the love of someone initially cold to warm up, your loving marriage encourages the members of your family to eventually love one another. Think about it. They wouldn't be family at all if you didn't fall in love as a couple in the first place. And without a committed, happy, ongoing relationship, children and extended family lose their motivation to be family to one another. Your coupleness is the first and last motivator for their familyness.

A number of studies show that the relational ties between stepfamily members correlate with the couple's relationship. Even after many years as a blended family, if a couple divorces, stepsiblings tend to lose contact with one another and far fewer adult stepchildren think it their obligation to care for an aging stepparent like they would a biological parent.[4] The permanence of your marriage is what keeps them at a minimum, motivated for a basic connection and at a maximum, defining one another as family.

By the way, we believe, based on a review of the research on cohabitation, that married couples make the strongest statement of permanence to their children and extended family. Cohabitation cannot match this. Why should children and extended family find room in their heart to love and appreciate a stepparent or embrace an adult stepsibling if their parent has left the door open to leaving the one relationship that has brought everyone together?

Couples and family members need clear definition of the future in order to find their motivation for familyness. Your relationship is what makes that happen.

Principle #4: Parents in blended families have to be a team and play to their individual strengths.

Parenting in the stepfamily ocean has inherent challenges so it requires synchronized swimming by parents. In most stepfamilies this includes two groups: the parent and stepparent within your home and the co-parents in separate homes. Essentially, all the parental players need to see themselves as a team—and consider each other teammates. Each has to accept the involvement of the other, even if they didn't want them there in the first place, and on behalf of the children find ways of working together. Finding grace in your heart for all the members of the parenting team can be very difficult for some. The advantages for children are numerous, including having a more stable environment, not being caught in between-home battles, and having predictable boundaries, just to name a few.

> While later-life stepparents are not trying to function like a parent to adult stepchildren, they are still trying to build a relationship and navigate life together.

Playing to your individual strengths in part means recognizing that an insider biological parent can set boundaries with potency in a way an outsider stepparent can't. On the other hand, sometimes a stepparent, because they have been emotionally removed from everything that has happened in a child's life, can ask probing questions and comfort a child in a way a biological parent cannot. Every parenting role has pros and cons. The trick is being aware of these strengths in your other teammates and releasing control in order to let them play roles you cannot.

Principle #5: Loss complicates bonding and building love, so grieve well.

Stepfamilies are born out of losses that must be grieved over time. But since not everyone has experienced the same loss, family members need to learn to grieve together. The loss experienced by Kate and her three children, for example, could have been very different than the loss experienced by Chris and his two daughters. Or maybe they were similar (e.g., divorce), but varied widely in terms of emotional impact (a high-conflict divorce versus an amicable one). Whichever the case, loss and its accompanying grief journey are ongoing. A new marriage does not put a halt to sadness or hurt, and it certainly doesn't stop the recalibrations that loss brings. For example, children who before their parents' divorce thought that life was safe and predictable are recalibrated by loss into an awareness that bad things can and do happen. This in turn can complicate bonding with new family members. Children who watched their mom and dad fall out of love are no longer certain that love will last—or that the new family will last.

Given that grief is a powerful undercurrent in the stepfamily ocean, always just below the surface of daily interactions, both parents and stepparents should look for ways to share their grief journeys openly. For parents, recognizing sadness ("you're missing your mom today, huh") and entering a child's grief at holidays, special days, and milestone moments ("I know celebrating Christmas is hard without your mother") is important for the child's well-being and the process of family bonding. Grief must not be denied. Sharing the journey together is what makes grief tolerable.

Principle #6: Don't walk away too soon.

If part of your blended family isn't loving or safe, do what can be done. In the meantime, don't toss away or minimize the good you do have. Lean in to what is working, to what feels safe, and appreciate it. It might not feel like much, but don't allow struggles to cancel out joys.

We have observed that most stepcouples that divorce do so long before they ever experienced any of the rewards of their journey. They just quit too soon. You may not like something—or many somethings—in your family right now, but don't give up on all of it. The divorce rate for blended family couples is between 10 to 25 percent higher than first marriages.[5] But it doesn't have to be. We are convinced that smart stepfamilies who learn to speak love well can thrive in their journey and experience marital oneness and child well-being and break the generational cycle of divorce for future generations. When the going gets tough in your home, hold on to this hope. Keep learning and growing. Sacrifice a little more and love more deeply. Perseverance pays off.

Principle #7: Learning to love well comes by putting away guilt and knowing the source of love.

Stepfamilies and guilt seem to go hand in hand. It could be guilt based on actions, such as adultery, effectively ending a marriage and causing emotional wounds in children, or the passive guilt a partner feels because they were left by an ex (they didn't make the decision to leave, but feel they could have prevented it somehow). Spiritual shame or guilt over a past you can't change can be debilitating to some, especially if they are met with social judgment by their religious community. Not being able to take communion, or not being able to serve in the children's ministry due to being divorced, send repeated messages to people that they are tainted or unworthy. The person might then assume that God also holds them at arm's length.

Feeling spiritually dirty or second-class has a powerful depressing effect on one's psychological, physical, and relational well-being. A young man approached me (Ron) after church one day to ask what to me was a gut-wrenching question. He explained that his parents' marriage was the result of an affair that had ended each of their first marriages. He first wondered if their marriage was legitimate in the eyes of the church. Then he asked if he, being the fruit of that marriage, was acceptable in God's eyes. My heart sank for him. I assured him that indeed he was accepted by God and that God didn't view him as contaminated or of no value. I then shared with him that the love of God isn't based on our ability to earn it; it is freely offered. And more to the point, when disobedience is part of someone's past (his parents), I told him that with repentance God is quick to forgive.

Knowing that God sets you free, frees you to pass along His love and forgiveness to others in your home. Loving well comes by knowing the source of love.

Living and loving well in a blended family is a long, often challenging journey. Eventually, however, if you stick with it, you step into your destination. You want a good blend—the principles we just shared are a great first step. Next, let's look at the five love languages—and how to apply them to *your* blended family.

YOUR TURN

Make a list of each person in your blended family. Be sure to include important extended family members, grandparents, perhaps even biological parents not living in your home. What is the level of motivation toward love of each person? How do their definitions of what is loving within your blended family differ? And finally, discuss with someone which of the seven rules for loving well your family is excelling in and which needs some improvement.

2

Understanding the Languages of Love

EVERYONE WANTS to be loved—needs to be loved. And everyone needs *to* love. Sounds simple, right? Well, not so much. Because, as you will see, not everyone gives, receives or understands love in the same way. Here is a quick guide to the five love languages. For some, it will be a refresher; for others, a new and possibly transformative concept.

LIFE-GIVING LOVE

Mature love is selfless in nature; it serves and considers the needs of others first. It chooses to sacrifice on the other's behalf and seeks to know the other person intimately. This kind of love requires humility, intentionality, and personal discipline. Humility, to remain teachable and not think more highly of yourself than the other; intentionality, to give careful consideration to what will be most loving to the person; and discipline, to regulate one's thoughts and feelings, especially during times of relationship uncertainty, in order to act in loving ways.

Being loved in this way, in a consistent manner, is life-giving for both children and adults. It adds to our sense of value and worth, makes us feel safe and secure, and inspires us to love others in a similar manner. That's why *how we love* is so important. A well-intentioned love that misses the mark may not strengthen the relationship or even communicate love—and an inconsistent or unreliable love won't foster safety or trust that love will last.[1] We must be intentional, in the best manner, in order to love and, ultimately, be loved well.

The concept of intentional love has become both a belief and an action for many people as they have gained an understanding of the five love languages. If you've read one of The 5 Love Languages books, maybe you have used its simple yet profound message to transform a relationship of your own. If you are not already familiar with the love languages, we encourage you to read or listen to one of the books (see the list on page 6 for the titles).

A QUICK GUIDE TO THE FIVE LOVE LANGUAGES[2]

Whether you are familiar with the love languages or not, before we apply them in the context of blended family, here's a brief recap to give us all a common framework: Imagine how difficult it would be to communicate with someone from China if you did not know a word of Chinese and he did not know a word of English. You could draw pictures, use Google translator, or physically act out your message, but to really communicate effectively, at least one of you would have to learn to speak the other person's language. In *The 5 Love Languages*, I (Gary) use the metaphor of literal languages to help readers understand that the ways individuals perceive emotional love are so distinct from one another that they essentially comprise five different "languages" or channels of communication. Each of us has at least one language that communicates emotional love to us more deeply than the others. This is called your primary love language. The next most clear language is your secondary language.

The five love languages are:

Words of Affirmation: *Words that speak to the worth of the individual.* One of the "dialects" of this love language is a heartfelt compliment. These may focus on something about how the person looks, or on some personality trait, or something they have done. Examples: "You did a really good job on that project." "I appreciate your truthfulness with me." "You look nice in that outfit." Another dialect is words of encouragement, such as: "You almost made it. I know if you keep trying you will be great at basketball." Another is words of praise. These should always focus on "effort" and not "perfection." "You worked really hard on raking the leaves and I appreciate it." This love language may be spoken verbally, or in writing. The purpose is to affirm things you sincerely appreciate about the person. A "Words of Affirmation person" can be emotionally devastated by insults and harsh words.

Quality Time: *Giving someone your full, undivided attention.* This may involve meaningful conversations where you share thoughts, feelings, desires, or frustrations. The important thing is that you give your full attention to the other person when they are talking. You are looking at them, nodding your head, and trying to understand their perspective. Another dialect of Quality Time is sharing meaningful experiences: a walk in the park, playing a game together, going shopping together, doing a service project together. The important thing is not "what" you are doing, but "why" you are doing it—to spend time together. A "Quality Time person" can be hurt by halfhearted or distracted listening, or by repeatedly postponing promised time together.

Gifts (or Receiving Gifts): *Giving someone something meaningful to them.* The gift may be purchased, handmade, or found as you took a walk in the park. The gift says, "They were thinking about me when we were apart." The gift need not be expensive. It really is "the thought that counts." It is the thoughtfulness and effort behind a gift that sends the "I love you" message. It is universal to give gifts as an expression of love. For some people this is their primary love language. A "Gifts person" can be hurt by a forgotten anniversary or birthday, or left feeling empty in a relationship void of tangible tokens of love. For some, the physical presence of someone they care about is a manifestation of a gift, and they can be hurt when someone doesn't "show up" at an important time.

Acts of Service: *Doing things to help another person.* In a marriage this would include cooking meals, doing laundry, walking the dog, picking up a prescription, taking out the trash, mowing the grass, changing the baby's diaper. With children it is doing things for them that they cannot do for themselves, and then teaching them to do age-appropriate things for themselves (or others). To discover meaningful acts of service you might ask, for example, "Would it be helpful to you if I watered the plants?" Actions speak louder than words to those who have this love language. An "Acts of Service person" can be hurt by laziness, someone leaving a mess for them to clean up, or forgotten promises to help.

> "My adult stepchildren need acts of service and verbal encouragement. I try to keep in touch through email, phone calls, or texting. Whenever possible I try to affirm their family and offer to help with the kids or tasks around the house."

Physical Touch: Connecting with someone physically. We have long known the emotional importance of touch. That is why we pick up babies, hold them and cuddle them. Long before the baby knows the meaning of the word *love*, the baby feels loved by physical touch. There are many expressions (dialects) of physical touch. "High fives," a pat on the shoulder, and sitting close to a person on the sofa are relatively easy ways to speak this love language. Other dialects require more time and effort, such as a foot massage, or a back rub. Still others require discernment as to how, when, and with whom you will share more intimate touches like hugs and kissing. Wrestling or playing games that require physical touch is another mode of expressing this language.

> Seldom do husbands and wives share the same love language.

For some people, physical touch communicates most clearly "I love you." For a "Physical Touch person," an angry shove or slap or other physical abuse can cause extreme emotional pain.

All of these are valid ways to express love to others. However, what makes one person feel loved does not necessarily make another person feel loved. We each have a primary love language—one that speaks most deeply to us. Seldom do husbands and wives share the same love language. If you have three children, they may have three different love languages. By nature we tend to show our love to others by speaking our own love language (the one that is most meaningful to us). When we do this, we may be sincere, but the other person may not feel loved.

The key is learning to speak the other person's love language. It may be a language that is not comfortable to you, one that you did not learn to speak growing up. But if you want the person to genuinely feel loved, you must first of all discover their primary love language and then choose to speak it on a regular basis. This will take time and effort, but the relationship rewards are well worth the effort. When two people mutually embrace this concept and are speaking each other's love language, the relationship flourishes.

THE FIVE LOVE LANGUAGES AND BLENDED FAMILIES

However, what if both individuals in a relationship don't mutually embrace the idea of the love languages or value the connection they might receive by doing so? What if one insider wants to keep an outsider out? What if someone cares for a stepfamily member and wants to speak their love language, but doing so jeopardizes their relationship with someone else they deeply love and are loyal to? In the next chapter we'll discuss in detail common blended family barriers to speaking the love languages and what you can do about them. For now, let's focus on relationships where both people are open to one another and how you can be ready to speak their language.

Be intentional

It takes intentionality to learn a new language, excel in your job, or change your diet. Learning someone's love language requires the same. Intentional "lovers" share some common attributes. For example, they possess self-awareness, strive to be trustworthy, and seek to observe and deeply *know* the person they love. This "knowing" includes recognizing how the other reacts when not feeling loved or safe. If you want to be an "intentional lover," learn the primary and secondary love languages of that individual—and express love accordingly.

It's interesting, but sometimes the obvious eludes us. In a survey of stepcouples that were familiar with the five love languages, 6 percent had not tried to apply them to the relationships in their home. Now, that doesn't mean they don't care for their family; they just hadn't become intentional about putting knowledge into action. I (Ron) have many tools in my garage toolbox, but I usually use the ones with which I'm most familiar even if another would be better suited for the job. (Which, by the way, was always a mystery to my jack-of-all-trades father-in-law, whom I highly respected. He tried to help me. Oh, how he tried.)

Take a minute to ponder which relational "tools" you utilize most often. When it comes to your couple relationship do you attempt to move toward the other with kind words, or do you prefer a more indirect approach, hoping it will pull them in closer? And what is your dance move when there's tension between you: toward or away, vocal or silent? And what about with children and/or stepchildren? What are your most commonly used relational tools to help them mature or to grow your relationship? Self-awareness is important because you might have another tool right in front of you that is better suited for the job at hand—you just have to become intentional enough to see it and pick it up. When asked how she had made use of her knowledge of the love languages in her blended family one stepparent said, "I haven't tried to speak my stepkids' love language. I guess I'm just trying to love them the way I love my daughter." She thought a minute and said, "Maybe I should be more intentional than that."

Look around. You may find another tool nearby that could be very useful.

In the beginning and over time

All relationships have seasons when intentionality is easier and when it is more difficult. Have you noticed, for example, that we voluntarily act more loving and kind—and are quick to make sacrifices—at the beginning of a romantic relationship? New romantic love—otherwise known as infatuation—captivates us and motivates us to do things we would never do if we were not "in love." (Maybe that's why many songs of every genre are about falling in love, not the long-term maintenance of a loving relationship.) But we don't mind. And we don't mind making all the sacrifices needed to pursue the relationship. Why? Because we're *in love*.

> Intentionality wanes when infatuation wears off.

Intentionality is easy when we're infatuated because we're highly motivated. The problem is, intentionality wanes when infatuation wears off. For example, I've (Ron) joked for many years that men are hunters when it comes to falling in love. We spot what we hope will be our future wife and systematically go about chasing her heart until we've captured it. But once a ring is on her finger, we've caught our limit, so to speak, and don't try as hard anymore. Instead, we hunt other things, like a career, or a man cave, or becoming a video game champion.

This, of course, is a setup for both him and his bride. Before marriage she came to believe he cherished her (which he did); his intentionality communicated a deep commitment and passion for her. When he shifts his hunting energy elsewhere, she becomes disillusioned and hurt. He then feels her disappointment and perhaps anger, but is confused because in his heart he is still just as much in love with her as before. In short, the decrease in intentionality fosters insecurity and discouragement in the marriage.

A similar dynamic occurs when a couple with children from a previous relationship starts dating. The man and woman are intentional to date each other (developing what I like to call *coupleness*[3]) and perhaps one another's children (working toward *familyness*). However, at some point they begin to take one or the other relationship, usually the children, for granted. "Her kids and I seemed to get along just fine while we were dating," one man said. "Neither of us expected them to cry during the wedding like they did." Infatuation with each other lulled them to sleep regarding their children. They might have seen the signs or symptoms before the wedding, but they just weren't looking.

By the way, assuming "because I love their mom/dad the kids will warm up to me" rarely proves to be the case. Kids (of all ages) have their own opinions about who they like and certainly who they love. They need to feel safe before they will embrace you. Don't think you can short-circuit the process just by loving their parent.

And don't assume that because your "stepchild" is an adult, he or she won't have powerful feelings about you dating or marrying their parent. One man naively said, "My stepson is an adult; I haven't even tried to figure out what his love language is." They may look and sound a little different, but adult children have just as many emotional transitions and life adjustments to make when a parent marries as minor aged children do.

Any valued relationship requires intentional effort at the beginning and over time. You must never assume otherwise.

What about you? Has your intentionality waned?

KNOW YOUR OWN LOVE LANGUAGES

Earlier we pointed out that for most of us, our first instinct is to love others using our primary love language. That is, we know how it makes us feel so we naturally assume that is what will make someone else feel our love. In other words, it's possible to be intentional but misguided in your efforts. Identifying your own primary (and secondary) love language helps you guard against assuming what will communicate love.

Candace and her two kids were huggers. They hugged each other multiple times each day. They hugged to say hello, goodbye, I'm sorry, how was your day, thank you, and goodnight, sleep-tight. They even hugged strangers. When asked what physical touch meant to her, Candace would say, "Warmth. You belong. And love."

It's no surprise, then, that Candace was physical from the start with her husband and stepchildren. Only her stepchildren weren't receptive. They bristled when she tried to hug them. Candace's intentions were good and her desire to connect appropriate, but her strategy was misguided because it was based on her love language and what she and her children shared, not what spoke best to her stepchildren. Her timing was off, too. In the next chapter we'll explain that even if one of her stepchildren's love language was Physical Touch, Candace should move slowly toward it because physical touch is inherently intimate and needs a strong foundation of trust before it can be received as it was intended.

Recognizing what speaks love to others may be different from what communicates love to you—and finding the willingness to speak their language—may uncover a layer of selfishness in you. It did in me (Ron).

Early in our marriage I tried to be intentional in loving Nan.

Occasionally I would plan a special evening or surprise to let her know how much I cared. Most of the time these efforts were well received, but when they were not I usually pouted or got irritated with her. What I eventually discovered about myself (boy did it take a long time) was an attitude that needed an adjustment. Essentially I was saying to Nan, "I've calculated how I'll demonstrate my love and expect you to be okay with that. Nothing more, nothing less. I'll love you my way."

We think a great many people make that mistake. We calculate how much love we're willing to give and the manner in which we'll give it, and then insist that nothing else be expected of us. But maturing lovers let love teach them what sacrifices are required and what language they need to speak. If we insist on loving others in a predetermined way rather than speaking their love language, our efforts will miss the mark. They will not feel loved. We must be open to learning a love language that may not be comfortable or natural to us if we are to be successful lovers.

CAN I TRUST YOU?

Our decades of combined experience training therapists, speaking at conferences, and educating stepfamilies has taught us that one of the most overlooked and underestimated needs of any relationship is the need for trustworthiness. To be able to count on someone—to know them as reliable, responsible, and dependable—is imperative.[4]

If you've ever been in a relationship with someone who was inconsistent toward you, unpredictable in whether they were mindful of you, or unreliable to keep their promises, you know how important trust is. Without it, the words of love, even the actions of love, lose meaning.

Being trustworthy simply means that you act with integrity

toward the person and that you strive to honor your commitments to them and the relationship. Basically, you put your money where your mouth is. This, in turn, fosters safety in the relationship and, generally speaking, trust (though it doesn't guarantee it).

Some relationships naturally carry a foundation of trust, and others don't. Biological relationships between parents and children, for example, have a measure of built-in trust, which is why kids naturally entrust themselves to the leadership of their parents and freely forgive when parents apologize. This is also why we assume our kids are telling us the truth about how Mrs. Jones's window got broken. You could say trust comes automatically when you share DNA. For example, a mom may disagree with how her husband handles a parenting moment, but she doesn't accuse him of despising their child. It would take a lot of evidence to the contrary for her to come to believe that.

> Without trust, the words, even the actions of love, lose meaning.

The point is this: the natural grace offered to those we consider family creates a divide in blended families. Family members related by blood naturally trust each other more than stepparents or stepsiblings and are more willing to accommodate one another's needs. They are also much more likely to tolerate irritating personality quirks, forgive one another when disappointed, and make the effort to repair a damaged relationship. This difference will get more attention later in the book, but recognize that the first solution is always acting in a trustworthy manner, especially with those who don't naturally trust you. Consistent trustworthiness eventually builds trust—and with it, an openness to you speaking their love language.

LEARN THEIR DIALECT

As in spoken languages, each of the love languages has different dialects. Understanding dialects helps you speak the love languages more effectively. For example, Steve read *The 5 Love Languages* book during his first marriage. As it turns out, his first wife, Audrey, and second wife, Laura, both have the same Quality Time love language, but their dialect is very different. Steve can sit quietly with Laura and watch a TV program, for example, and she considers that quality time. However, just sitting beside each other was not sufficient for his first wife, who needed direct eye contact and interaction for her to experience love. It took Steve a while to recognize Laura's slight dialect differences, but once he did, they have enjoyed the outcome.

One father said, "I knew that my eleven-year-old son's love language was Physical Touch. A back rub would fill his love tank immediately. When I married Julie, a few years after my wife died, she told me that her ten-year-old son's love language was Physical Touch. So naturally I thought, 'I'll give him a back rub.' However, when I tried, he made it clear that he did not like back rubs. After talking with Julie I started giving him high fives and shoulder bumps. He received them with a smile. That's when I learned the importance of speaking the right dialect."

Dialects are often discovered by trial and error. First, we must discover the primary love language of each person in the blended family. Then we explore the various ways (dialects) to express that language.

RECOGNIZE CULTURAL DISTINCTIVES

Sometimes in intercultural blended families, learning to speak another's language literally means learning to speak their language. Spoken language and cultural differences (like traditions, social mores, and family role expectations) add another significant "language barrier" to some blended families. It may also confuse your understanding of someone's love language. Some cultures are more gregarious and physical, for example, in how they greet one another or show affection. Observing this in someone does not necessarily mean his or her love language is Physical Touch. Be a student of one another's cultural distinctives and help children understand the differences to aid in the process of bonding and accepting one another.

For example, the role definitions of a Caucasian woman raised to be her own independent woman may clash with those of her Hispanic husband raised in a strong machismo culture. His idea of his role as a new stepdad may differ greatly from hers (see chapter 5 for stepparent prescriptions), but doesn't mean either's cultural heritage is "wrong." However, they will need to merge their expectations and find a common path if they are going to merge their families. It is likely they will need to have many conversations about this to find common ground.

Cultural expectations can affect extended family relationships as well. One man said his Irish American family is so close they often keep former in-laws in the family even after divorce. This open boundary felt uncomfortable to his new wife whose extended family and cultural heritage would never do that.

To manage cultural differences and differentiate them from love languages, coach children about differences and how to respond ahead of time. Knowing before spending time with new stepgrandparents or extended family members that someone will bow when greeted instead of shaking their hand lessens a child's confusion when it happens. It can also create a curiosity and respect for the person's culture that opens the door to relationship, not judgment.

Using obvious differences as fun opportunities to teach and train children is another good idea. Looking at family photos or discussing clothing styles or foods prepared at holidays and special days can reveal cultural beliefs and family history. Have fun eating the meal and discussing what it represents.

Finally, blending an intercultural family may require that you examine your family cultural patterns and ask if they are still functional for your new family. A mother who—along with the three generations of mothers before her—has played the role of both mother and father in her family, may have a hard time letting her new husband find his place as stepfather in the home. It's not so much that she is refusing to let him in or that she's trying to "emasculate him," as she is struggling not to play the role she knows and expects of herself. Doing so may have been functional until now, but going forward, she will likely need to make space for him to step into the family.

KNOW YOURSELF WHEN FEELING UNLOVED

All of us feel unloved or emotionally unsafe at some point in any close relationship. What we do with that feeling is important because our response can either help restore security or make the situation worse.

Every time Alejandro's wife and stepchildren started telling funny stories that predated his involvement in their life, he felt left out. And at times it felt like his stepchildren were intentionally reminding him he didn't belong.

When it comes to stressful situations like this we all pretty much have a go-to set of coping behaviors—actions we take to try to deal with what's happening or change the circumstances so we don't feel vulnerable or unloved anymore.[5] One of Alejandro's go-to reactions is withdrawing in order to find emotional safety. His daughter, who was always willing to hang out with her daddy, was just such a place. He would go upstairs to her bedroom or TV room and they would play games, watch movies, or talk. Over time a pattern developed. Alejandro and his daughter avoided issues together upstairs while his wife and stepchildren huddled together downstairs.

Do you know what you typically do when feeling unloved or emotionally unsafe? If not, start taking notice. Strive for coping behavior that is constructive. When feeling disconnected, for example, gently articulating your desire for more connection (rather than doing so in anger) and patiently talking with them about how you might get more time together generally fosters mutual steps toward one another. But a harsh reaction that accuses, cuts the other person(s), and storms out of the room just makes it more likely that the disconnection will persist.

Yes, you feel unloved. But if you make it worse with your reaction, you're now part of the problem. You must recognize your part of the dance and manage it well.

BE GENUINE

Are you a salesman—or a genuine lover of your spouse, children, and stepchildren? A good salesman makes you believe they are your best friend, that they're looking out for you and have your interests in mind even when they just want you to buy something.

You can misuse the love languages by turning them into a tool of manipulation. We strongly advise you not to. Instead, let your effort to speak another person's language flow from a genuine desire in your heart to care for them. Speaking their language may take great effort and may not feel authentic because it's not your natural language, but that's the point: surrendering your preference in order to connect to the heart of the other is a genuine act of love.

But what if you're trying to grow your love for a new stepfamily member, but just don't feel it yet? Acts of love often precede feelings of love. For decades, we have witnessed stepparents selflessly choosing to love a child who is closed toward them. In the face of what feels like rejection, they choose to love. The good news is, this kind of love is compelling to both persons. Though they may not feel it in the beginning, the stepparent who initially loves in this way usually grows to really feel it—and often so does the child.

> "We have five kids altogether. It's taken years, but I finally understand their personalities and how God designed them; each is unique and adds something wonderful to our blended family. Without each of them I would have missed out on the joy and blessing they bring to my life."

It's not always natural to love every stepfamily member. Let's face it, some people are easier to love than others and some take great intentional effort to love. In either case, making the choice to love is a genuine starting point that can move both persons toward loving one another. Discovering their love language and starting to love them in that way is a significant first—and middle—step.

WISE AND PATIENT LOVE

Blended families start out looking and functioning very differently than biological families. The good news is that as family members bond and create a shared family identity over time, stepfamilies start functioning and feeling more and more like biological families. What happens between these two seasons—what we might call the "integration years"—either makes or breaks the family. In the beginning the insider/outsider dynamic fosters an inertia that is difficult to overcome, especially if, as we noted earlier, one stepfamily member isn't interested in giving or receiving love to another. "I am still being very careful to apply the love languages as we just got married a few months ago," said one stepparent. "The boys are still very reluctant to come close to me."

However, we are convinced: love that hits the bull's-eye of other people's hearts (the foundation of the five love languages) combined with the proven principles of Smart Stepfamilies can help you overcome the inertia. Healthy bonding, wise stepparenting, realistic expectations, and patient love will build bridges of mercy and grace that traverse territorial divides and likely connect the hearts of those in your stepfamily. As the stepparent above indicated, knowing when and *when not* to love a child with their primary love language is important. That brings us to chapter three and a discussion of when loves compete.

TAKE THE PROFILE

*Before continuing, now is the time to identify your primary
love language, your spouse's, and your family members.' Remember,
every person benefits from giving and receiving each of the love
languages, but knowing both their primary and secondary language
helps you to be an informed, mature lover. The following pages
include The 5 Love Languages Profile for Couples (for Him and for
Her), Teens, and of Children. We suggest you and your children take
the time to do each of them before reading further. Notice that your
children will take the profile multiple times while thinking about their
Dad and Mom, and if appropriate, Stepdad and/or Stepmom. This is
a great opportunity for you to see the differences in how they want
to receive love from various adults. The next chapter will help you
understand this further. If your children are unable or unwilling to
take the profile, the end of chapter 5 provides some guidelines for
discovering your child's love language.*

LOVE LANGUAGES PERSONAL PROFILE
FOR COUPLES

Below you will see 30 paired statements. Please circle the letter next to the statement that best defines what is most meaningful to you in your relationship. Both statements may (or may not) sound like they fit your situation, but please choose the statement that captures the essence of what is most meaningful to you, the majority of the time. Allow 10 to 15 minutes to complete the profile. Take it when you are relaxed, and try not to rush through it. If you prefer to use the free interactive version of this profile online, please visit 5lovelanguages.com.

It's more meaningful to me when . . .

1

I receive a loving note/text/email for no special reason from my loved one.	A
My partner and I hug.	E

2

I can spend alone time with my partner—just the two of us.	B
My partner does something practical to help me out.	D

3

My partner gives me a little gift as a token of our love for each other.	C
I get to spend uninterrupted leisure time with my partner.	B

4

My partner unexpectedly does something for me like filling my car with gas or doing the laundry.	D
My partner and I touch.	E

5

My partner puts his/her arm around me when we're in public.	E
My partner surprises me with a gift.	C

6

I'm around my partner, even if we're not really doing anything.	B
I hold hands with my partner.	E

7 My partner gives me a gift.   C

I hear "I love you" from my partner.   A

8 I sit close to my partner.   E

I am complimented by my loved one for no apparent reason.   A

9 I get the chance to just "hang out" with my partner.   B

I unexpectedly get small gifts from my partner.   C

10 I hear my partner tell me, "I'm proud of you."   A

My partner helps me with a task.   D

11 I get to do things with my partner.   B

I hear supportive words from my partner.   A

12 My partner does things for me instead of just talking about doing nice things.   D

I feel connected to my partner through a hug.   E

13 I hear praise from my partner.   A

My partner gives me something that shows he/she was really thinking about me.   C

14 I'm able to just be around my partner.   B

I get a back rub or massage from my partner.   E

15 My partner reacts positively to something I've accomplished.   A

My partner does something for me that I know she doesn't particularly enjoy.   D

16 My partner and I kiss frequently.   E

I sense my partner is showing interest in the things I care about.   B

17 My partner works on special projects with me that I have to complete.   D

My partner gives me an exciting gift.   C

18	I'm complimented by my partner on my appearance.	A
	My partner takes the time to listen to me and really understand my feelings.	B
19	My partner and I share nonsexual touch in public.	E
	My partner offers to run errands for me.	D
20	My partner does a bit more than his/her normal share of the responsibilities we share (around the house, work-related, etc.).	D
	I get a gift that I know my partner put thought into choosing.	C
21	My partner doesn't check his/her phone while we're talking.	B
	My partner goes out of their way to do something that relieves pressure on me.	D
22	I can look forward to a holiday because of a gift I anticipate receiving.	C
	I hear the words "I appreciate you" from my partner.	A
23	My partner brings me a little gift after he/she has been traveling without me.	C
	My partner takes care of something I'm responsible to do but I feel too stressed to do at the time.	D
24	My partner doesn't interrupt me while I'm talking.	B
	Gift giving is an important part of our relationship.	C
25	My partner helps me out when he/she knows I'm already tired.	D
	I get to go somewhere while spending time with my partner.	B
26	My partner and I are physically intimate.	E
	My partner gives me a little gift that he/she picked up in the course of her normal day.	C
27	My partner says something encouraging to me.	A
	I get to spend time in a shared activity or hobby with my partner.	B

28	My partner surprises me with a small token of her appreciation.	C
	My partner and I touch a lot during the normal course of the day.	E

29	My partner helps me out—especially if I know they're already busy.	D
	I hear my partner specifically tell me, "I appreciate you."	A

30	My partner and I embrace after we've been apart for a while.	E
	I hear my partner say how much I mean to him/her.	A

Now go back and count the number of times you circled each individual letter, and write that number in the appropriate blank below.

RESULTS

A: _____ WORDS OF AFFIRMATION

B: _____ QUALITY TIME

C: _____ RECEIVING GIFTS

D: _____ ACTS OF SERVICE

E: _____ PHYSICAL TOUCH

Which love language received the highest score? This is your primary love language. If point totals for two love languages are equal, you are "bilingual" and have two primary love languages. And, if you have a secondary love language, or one that is close in score to your primary love language, this means that both expressions of love are important to you. The highest possible score for any single love language is 12.

You're going to see 30 pairs of things that your parent(s) might do or say to show love to you. In the columns that apply to you, pick one item in each pair that you like better and circle it. For some of them, you might like both options—but just pick one. Allow 10 to 15 minutes to complete the profile. Take it when you are relaxed, and try not to rush through it. When you finish marking your answers, count how many times you circled each letter and transfer to the appropriate blank at the end of the test. If you prefer, take the interactive profile online at 5lovelanguages.com.

		DAD	MOM	STEPDAD	STEPMOM
1	Asks me what I think	A	A	A	A
	Puts his/her arm around my shoulder	E	E	E	E
2	Goes to my sports events, recitals, etc.	B	B	B	B
	Does my laundry	D	D	D	D
3	Buys me clothes	C	C	C	C
	Watches TV or movies with me	B	B	B	B
4	Helps me with school projects	D	D	D	D
	Hugs me	E	E	E	E
5	Kisses me on the cheek	E	E	E	E
	Gives me money for things I need	C	C	C	C
6	Takes time off of work to do stuff with me	B	B	B	B
	Rubs my shoulders or back	E	E	E	E
7	Gives me cool things for my birthday	C	C	C	C
	Reassures me when I fail or mess up	A	A	A	A

		DAD	MOM	STEPDAD	STEPMOM
8	Gives me a high five	E	E	E	E
	Respects my opinions	A	A	A	A
9	Goes out to eat or shops with me	B	B	B	B
	Lets me use his/her stuff	C	C	C	C
10	Tells me I'm the best son/daughter in the world	A	A	A	A
	Drives me to places I need to go	D	D	D	D
11	Eats at least one meal with me most every day	B	B	B	B
	Listens to me and helps me work through problems	A	A	A	A
12	Doesn't invade my privacy	D	D	D	D
	Holds or shakes my hand	E	E	E	E
13	Leaves me encouraging notes	A	A	A	A
	Knows what my favorite store is	C	C	C	C
14	Hangs out with me sometimes	B	B	B	B
	Sits next to me on the couch	E	E	E	E
15	Tells me how proud he/she is of me	A	A	A	A
	Cooks meals for me	D	D	D	D
16	Straightens my collar, necklace, etc.	E	E	E	E
	Shows interest in stuff that I'm interested in	B	B	B	B
17	Allows my friends to hang out at our house	D	D	D	D
	Pays for me to go on school or church trips	C	C	C	C
18	Tells me I look good	A	A	A	A
	Listens to me without judging me	B	B	B	B

	DAD	MOM	STEPDAD	STEPMOM
19 Touches or rubs my head	E	E	E	E
Sometimes lets me pick out where we go on family trips	D	D	D	D
20 Takes me to the doctor, dentist, etc.	D	D	D	D
Trusts me to be at home alone	C	C	C	C
21 Takes me on trips with him/her	B	B	B	B
Takes me and my friends to movies, concerts, etc.	D	D	D	D
22 Gives me stuff that I really like	C	C	C	C
Notices when I do something good	A	A	A	A
23 Gives me extra spending money	C	C	C	C
Asks me if I need help	D	D	D	D
24 Doesn't interrupt me when I'm talking	B	B	B	B
Likes the gifts I buy for him/her	C	C	C	C
25 Lets me sleep in late sometimes	D	D	D	D
Seems to really enjoy spending time with me	B	B	B	B
26 Pats me on the back	E	E	E	E
Buys me stuff and surprises me with it	C	C	C	C
27 Tells me he/she believes in me	A	A	A	A
Can ride in the car with me without lecturing me	B	B	B	B
28 Picks up stuff that I need from various stores	C	C	C	C
Sometimes holds or touches my face	E	E	E	E
29 Gives me some space when I'm feeling upset or angry	D	D	D	D
Tells me that I'm talented or special	A	A	A	A

	DAD	MOM	STEPDAD	STEPMOM
Hugs or kisses me at least once every day	E	E	E	E
Says he/she is thankful that I'm his/her child/stepchild	A	A	A	A

Now go back and count the number of times you circled each individual letter and write that number in the appropriate blank below.

RESULTS (DAD)

A: _____ WORDS OF AFFIRMATION

B: _____ QUALITY TIME

C: _____ RECEIVING GIFTS

D: _____ ACTS OF SERVICE

E: _____ PHYSICAL TOUCH

RESULTS (MOM)

A: _____ WORDS OF AFFIRMATION

B: _____ QUALITY TIME

C: _____ RECEIVING GIFTS

D: _____ ACTS OF SERVICE

E: _____ PHYSICAL TOUCH

RESULTS (STEPDAD)

A: _____ WORDS OF AFFIRMATION

B: _____ QUALITY TIME

C: _____ RECEIVING GIFTS

D: _____ ACTS OF SERVICE

E: _____ PHYSICAL TOUCH

RESULTS (STEPMOM)

A: _____ WORDS OF AFFIRMATION

B: _____ QUALITY TIME

C: _____ RECEIVING GIFTS

D: _____ ACTS OF SERVICE

E: _____ PHYSICAL TOUCH

WHICH LOVE LANGUAGE RECEIVED THE HIGHEST SCORE?

This is your primary love language. If point totals for two love languages are equal, you are "bilingual" and have two primary love languages. And, if you have a secondary love language, or one that is close in score to your primary love language, this means that both expressions of love are important to you. The highest possible score for any single love language is 12.

THE 5 love LANGUAGES
The Secret to Love That Lasts

LOVE LANGUAGES MYSTERY GAME
FOR CHILDREN

To Get Started:

Each clue box has two comments that parents sometimes make to their children. **Read each clue box and, of the two comments, pick the one you like better and wish your mom or dad would say to you.** *Then circle the letter that goes with that comment. Be careful and only circle one letter in each clue box! After you've gone through all 20 clue boxes, go back and count how many A's, B's, C's, D's, and E's that you circled. Then write your scores in the blanks at the end of the game. Ask your mom or dad for help if you have any questions. And have fun unlocking the love languages mystery! If you prefer, take the interactive profile online at 5lovelanguages.com.*

		DAD	MOM	STEPDAD	STEPMOM
1	Give me a hug!	A	A	A	A
	You are terrific!	B	B	B	B
2	I've got a special birthday present for you!	C	C	C	C
	I'll help you with your project.	D	D	D	D
3	Let's go to a movie.	E	E	E	E
	Give me a high five!	A	A	A	A
4	You are so smart!	B	B	B	B
	Have you made your Christmas list?	C	C	C	C
5	Would you help me cook dinner?	D	D	D	D
	I like going to fun places with you!	E	E	E	E
6	Give me a kiss!	A	A	A	A
	You are #1!	B	B	B	B

		DAD	MOM	STEPDAD	STEPMOM
7	I've got a surprise for you.	C	C	C	C
	We can make something really cool.	D	D	D	D
8	Let's watch TV together!	E	E	E	E
	Tag, you're it!	A	A	A	A
9	You did a great job!	B	B	B	B
	You've earned a special surprise!	C	C	C	C
10	You can invite your friends.	D	D	D	D
	Let's go to your favorite restaurant.	E	E	E	E
11	I'm going to give you a big hug!	A	A	A	A
	You are an awesome kid!	B	B	B	B
12	I made your favorite food.	C	C	C	C
	I checked your homework, and it looks great!	D	D	D	D
13	You are fun to hang out with!	E	E	E	E
	I'll race you!	A	A	A	A
14	Wow! You did it!	B	B	B	B
	Check under your bed for a special present!	C	C	C	C
15	I cleaned your room for you.	D	D	D	D
	Let's play a game together.	E	E	E	E
16	Would you like for me to scratch your back?	A	A	A	A
	You can do it! Don't give up!	B	B	B	B
17	What would you like for your birthday?	C	C	C	C
	We can pick up your friend on the way to the movie.	D	D	D	D

		DAD	MOM	STEPDAD	STEPMOM
18	I always like doing stuff with you.	E	E	E	E
	You are so huggable!	A	A	A	A
19	How did you know how to do that? You are brilliant!	B	B	B	B
	I can't wait to give you your present!	C	C	C	C
20	Don't worry! I'll pick you up on time!	D	D	D	D
	Let's spend the day doing whatever you want to do!	E	E	E	E

A's

- **How many A's did you circle for Dad?** _____
- **How many for Mom?** _____
- **How many for Stepdad?** _____
- **How many for Stepmom?** _____

A's stand for physical touch. People whose love language is Physical Touch like to receive hugs, kisses, and high fives.

B's

- **How many B's did you circle for Dad?** _____
- **How many for Mom?** _____
- **How many for Stepdad?** _____
- **How many for Stepmom?** _____

B's stand for words of affirmation. People whose love language is Words of Affirmation like for others to use words to tell them that they are special and that they do a good job.

C's

- **How many C's did you circle for Dad?** _____
- **How many for Mom?** _____
- **How many for Stepdad?** _____
- **How many for Stepmom?** _____

C's stand for gifts. People with the love language of Gifts feel good when someone gives them a special present or surprise.

D's

- **How many D's did you circle for Dad?** _____
- **How many for Mom?** _____
- **How many for Stepdad?** _____
- **How many for Stepmom?** _____

D's stand for acts of service. A person whose love language is Acts of Service likes it when others do nice things for them such as helping with chores, helping with school projects, or driving them places.

E's

- **How many E's did you circle for Dad?** _____
- **How many for Mom?** _____
- **How many for Stepdad?** _____
- **How many for Stepmom?** _____

E's stand for quality time. People with the love language of Quality Time like it when others do things with them like play a game, watch television, or go to a ball game.

To Solve the Love Language Mystery:

Look at your scores. The highest score represents your primary love language—how you most like to receive love. This doesn't mean the others aren't important, it just means that this is your favorite.

CONGRATULATIONS!

You've solved the love language mystery game and discovered your love language. Good job! Make sure to share the results with your parents.

When Loves Compete and Conflict

WE'VE ALREADY SAID a lot about building love in blended families—and how the five love languages help make that happen. Now we need to go deep into an issue we might call "compete and conflict."

"WHO DO YOU LOVE MORE?"

Blended family relationships naturally create loyalty conflicts—or maybe we could call them *love* conflicts. "Am I still loved? Who do you love more—your spouse/kids or me? What do you love more, your old life or *our* new one?" What results is a household of competing relationships where everyone is fighting to matter—to someone, but not necessarily everyone.

Angela's primary love language is Quality Time. Her two youngest kids also have Quality Time as their love language. So she naturally invested a lot of time and attention in her children, especially after the divorce. A simple nighttime ritual, lying in bed at night and talking about the day, took on great significance when she became a single parent. It served as a point of connection, grieving, and care for one another. Multiple nights a week she and her kids would spend at least thirty minutes, and often an hour and a half, talking about their feelings, telling stories, and comforting one another.

What was a source of comfort for her and the children became a source of competition and conflict when she married Anthony.

A single father of a girl and boy, Anthony was abandoned by his former wife with little notice. One day, she just up and left. For four years Anthony took care of everything, as his kids rarely saw their mother.

Finding each other was a dream come true for Anthony and Angela. They had many similar interests and shared values, and both saw in each other what they thought their children needed in a stepparent. While dating, Angie got lots of quality time from Anthony, especially when visitation took her kids to their dad's house for a few days. And Anthony, whose primary love language is Words of Affirmation, got lots of positive messages from Angela, who respected him as a father, provider, and business manager.

Once marriage moved the two families in together, Anthony appreciated the nightly ritual between Angie and her kids—at first. He kissed his kids goodnight and settled in to a TV show to relax while Angela spent quality time with her kids. He knew the ritual was important for her kids—and as an outsider, he knew not to infringe on their time—but soon he grew weary of the length of time his wife spent with them. At the end of the day he wanted a little of her, too, and frankly was offended she didn't save some of her time for him. Frequently, by the time she left the kids' bedrooms she was tired and just wanted to go to bed herself. Anthony felt cheated and unimportant—feelings that because of his ex-wife were all too familiar to him.

He tried to help Angela be more efficient with her time distribution. At work he was a quality control efficiency expert so he began coaching her on ways she could spend less time with them and more with him. "I'm not saying you can't spend any time with them, I'm just hoping you could cut it down to forty-five minutes."

But Angela believed the bedtime ritual provided stability for her young children who needed it "more than ever," given the stress of their new family. Plus, their kids' visitation schedules meant she spent more time with his kids during most weeks than with her own.

Anthony tried getting the kids to give their mom "permission" to be with him. He would stand outside their bedroom and make vague remarks implying "it was his time" to be with her. Her kids got the message, all right, but looked to their mom to protect their time and asked why he would try to change it. "Mom, why is he rushing you? Doesn't he care about us?" This in turn deepened Angie's commitment to protect her kids. It also frustrated her because she could see how Anthony was inadvertently pushing her children away.

At this rate, she feared, their family would never fully blend. Every time she tried to explain this to him and ask him to back off, he accused her of loving her kids more than she loved him. Consequently, Angela had fewer respectful words for him.

THE TRIANGLE OF ATTACHMENTS

What is happening here?

Everyone is fighting to be loved and feel safe.

This story illustrates the triangle of emotional attachments that is typical of blended families. Each side is competing for love (and in this case, time) with at least one other side of the triangle. Angela's relationship with her children is competing with her marriage to Anthony and vice versa. In addition, the conflict between those two sides is sabotaging the third side; that is, the relationship between Anthony and her kids. The "insiders" are struggling to trust the new "outsider" stepparent. The adults and children have different motivations to love. And even though Anthony knows that Quality Time is the best language for his wife, for him to speak it to her is to pull her away from her children and add to her feelings of guilt (a classic feeling in this situation).

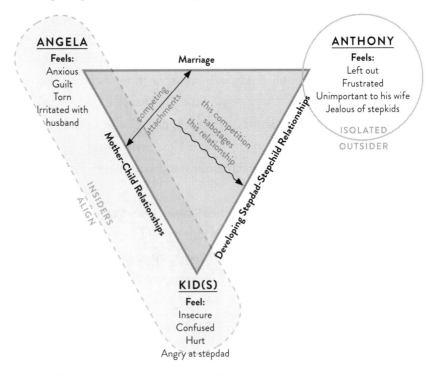

What Angela and Anthony did (and you can, too)

Before quality time can be shared, each side of the attachment triangle must make adjustments to their expectations of one another and be willing to change how they distribute time. And most importantly, each parent must protect their marriage from the resulting conflict and stress.

And that's where Angela and Anthony started.

Guard your marriage. The couple spent hours talking around and through this situation. They read books about stepfamily living and came to understand the many emotional dynamics involved for both them and their children. Being dedicated to this process and to listening openly to one another served a protective function for their marriage. It took months to see things improve, but their marital commitment and willingness to learn helped them endure the stress.

Consider others: empathy and compassion. Eventually both Anthony and Angela developed an empathy and compassion for everyone involved. Angie understood how not making time for her husband tapped into his pain of not being important to his first wife, and Anthony came to appreciate her parental guilt and need to protect her kids. And both of them developed a shared compassion for the kids' need for consistency and focused time with their mom.

Empathy sometimes opens a doorway to solutions not previously seen. Some solutions have to do with how we love others; while some focus on how we care for ourselves.

Remain calm. The first form of self-care both parents had to learn was to remain calm when another side of the triangle seemed to be getting more time or love. Anthony had to manage his fear that he would never get time with his wife and Angela had to deal with her worry that her children would emotionally fall apart unless she gave them an hour and a half of her time. Unless you're face-to-face with a bear, panic usually doesn't lead to healthy actions. Learning to manage your panic, your anxiety, your fear is a must in every intimate relationship. For then and only then can you objectively consider the needs of others.

Set boundaries and bless the connection. Once they began calming their panic, Anthony started valuing his wife's time with her kids and gave his blessing to their connection rather than resenting it. And Angela proactively began setting time limits on the nighttime ritual so she could save some of her quality time for her husband and offer more words of affirmation.

By the way, setting boundaries with her children in this manner will likely give Angie an opportunity to educate her kids about her dedication to her husband—and it may test her resolve. Children of all ages who have been through a series of painful family transitions naturally push back when a parent shifts their emotional energies toward a stepparent or other member of the stepfamily. Some kids get angry, some withdraw, others toss a guilt trip or the silent treatment hand grenade at their parent, but the competing-attachment message under this behavior is always the same: *Did I just lose you? If I did, please come back.* Angela had compassion for this emotional experience and anticipated it, so she knew what to do. She reassured her children that she still loved them—and had not gone anywhere—but in light of how their family had changed she did need to put a limit on how much time they spent hanging out at bedtime. And, in the case of her son, she eventually had to impose consequences for his disrespectful tone toward both her and Anthony.

> What kids need is your strong, comforting leadership, not your pity.

To make all this happen, Angela first had to push past her own guilt. Even before entering a stepfamily, kids have been through a lot. No parent ever wants their children to feel insecure or feel more pain. But the relational changes of blended families almost ensures they will. Angie recognized that she was often paralyzed by her guilt but found enough emotional resolve to push through and set appropriate boundaries anyway.

We tell parents doing this often results in more "weeping and gnashing of teeth" from children in the short-term, but eventually provides the stable environment they need. What your kids need in these moments is your strong comforting leadership, not your pity. They need you to remain connected and close even as you "disappoint" them.

Find balance in moving toward others. Initially, the best way to help a child move toward a stepparent is for the biological parent to first move toward the child. A child who has already lost a parent to death or divorce does not want to now lose connection with their biological parent who has fallen in love with another person. If your child feels you slipping away, they want more of you, not less. For you to demand indiscriminately that they move toward their stepparent (or future stepparent) is to ask them to "sleep with the enemy." Much better for you to first move toward them by speaking their primary love language so they feel your continued presence, while you also invest yourself in the new love relationship. Eventually, this makes loving a stepparent not a threat to the child's relationship with you.

This, of course, requires a careful balance of time and effort (and you may often feel split in two). A parent who indiscriminately throws himself or herself into a new love relationship fuels a child's sense of abandonment. Meanwhile, the stepparent who is trying to bond with a stepchild will likely find them hesitant or even closed altogether. Again, the biological parent must move toward their child while simultaneously developing and deepening their new couple relationship in order to reassure the child that their parent still values them and that their relationship—though altered—is not lost. This, paradoxically, makes it more likely that a stepchild will make space for their stepparent in their heart and eventually move toward them.

This is easier for biological parents to manage if the stepparent is patient. Stepparents need to acknowledge that they are, to a degree, taking the parent away from the children. Have compassion for this, and trust that blessing your spouse's time with their kids apart from you will eventually bless your marriage.

Encourage and bless connections with others. The parent-stepparent-child attachment triangle isn't the only triangle with competing relationships in blended families. The child-dad-stepdad and mom-stepmom triangles put children in the cruel position of loving each person without offending the other; they are most notably worried about losing favor with their biological parent. And there are triangles between grandparents, grandchildren, and stepgrandchildren, or a parent, their adult biological children, and the parent's new younger stepchildren. What is needed is permission to like or love everyone.

At the age of seven, Diego started calling his stepmom "*Madrastra*" (Spanish for "stepmom"), but his biological mother objected because it felt too endearing to her. She told him to stop and demanded that the boy's father and stepmom refuse to let him use that term in their home.

Sarah's husband had a foster son from a previous marriage that he continued to support financially. He had promised to help him

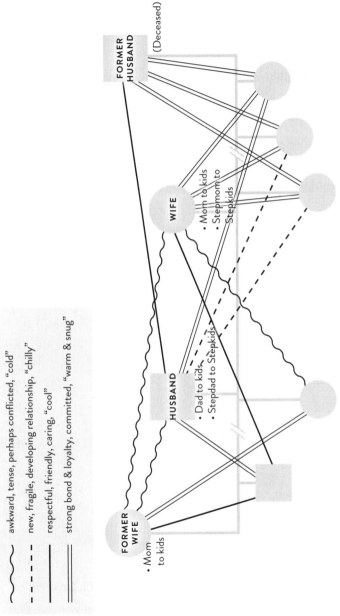

awkward, tense, perhaps conflicted, "cold"

new, fragile, developing relationship, "chilly"

respectful, friendly, caring, "cool"

strong bond & loyalty, committed, "warm & snug"

FORMER
HUSBAND

(Deceased)

WIFE

· Mom to kids
· Stepmom to
  Stepkids

HUSBAND

· Dad to kids
· Stepdad to Stepkids

FORMER
WIFE

· Mom
  to kids

BLENDED FAMILIES HAVE MULTIPLE, INTERLOCKING TRIANGLES

(This sample genogram shows that children and adults are part of many
relational triangles with relationships of varying "temperatures")

73

get through college, but Sarah objected. "He's not even your son. Why are you giving him money? Let's keep it for our family instead."

Triangle love conflicts get played out in many aspects of stepfamily life. Terms of endearment and money issues are common. But the heart of the matter is not about labels or dollar bills. Again, it's competing attachments. It is about wanting to be chosen and special to the ones you love. But the pursuit of emotional safety and security in a relationship does not require you to bash or distance the other party. Paradoxically, the way out is to encourage, even bless the appropriate connections others have with the ones they love. Encourage your spouse to spend agreed-upon money and balanced time with their child or children; your daughter to spend time with her stepparent; your later-life parent to spend energy investing in their new marriage. When you give your blessing to someone, it proves you are a safe, respectable, gracious, and trustworthy person, able to consider their needs above yours.

EXAMPLE: MOM AND STEPFATHER FAMILY

Children, in particular, need this gift from at least one person in their triangle—hopefully both! They naturally worry that someone else in their triangle will be offended or feel rejected if they love the other person too well. A parent's permission, even blessing, to connect with, like, be friendly toward, even love the other person(s) in the triangle is like taking them out of the middle of a boxing match between two heavyweight fighters. When a dad says to his children, "Have a good time with your stepdad this weekend," it frees them to be kids again, not miniature adults looking after their anxious father by being distant or disobedient to a stepfather. Or when a stepmother says, "I'm so excited you get to a have special birthday party with your mom next week," it communicates to the child that the two adults in this triangle are being adults, not petty seventh-graders trying to move up the social ladder on the backs of someone else. It says, "You are free to love without guilt or anxiety." Children—of every age—need this gift. Without it, they experience more pain.

PAIN AND LOSS

Blended families are formed as the result of painful circumstances for both children and adults: death, divorce, or the dissolution of a romantic relationship. Every blended family starts with a loss narrative. When new people enter that narrative, pain and grief confuse the process of bonding and muddy the waters of trust.

One stepmom said, "I was trying to bond with kids whose mother had died less than a year before. Much of our first dating experience felt like grief counseling. Then after we married, my oldest stepson went into a shell. Years later, he told us he had walls around his heart for seven years. There was little conversation and no getting through to him. His sisters now call me their 'bonus mom,' but initially they weren't polite or open to me at all.

"Much of our first dating experience felt like grief counseling."

Their mom was seldom sick, but when she got cancer she was gone in a couple months. It completely devastated the kids! For a few years they weren't open to me coming into their life."

Can you blame them? They're just kids having to deal with monumental loss. Grief of that magnitude has a way of recalibrating everything in your world and stealing joy from your life. Opening yourself to love new people and expending the necessary energy to create new relationships when the family you wanted is gone is an exhausting experience. And sometimes, kids just don't want to try.

Other kids hold out for what they've lost. Anthony's son, Jaylen, the younger of his two children, was five when his mother walked out of his life and nine when Angie and her kids walked in. Learning that his primary love language is Gifts, Angela tried to fill the gap in his life left by his mother. At first she resisted buying him gifts because she didn't want to be perceived as "buying his love," so she, being a Quality Time person, tried spending one on one time with Jaylen. The only problem: he didn't want to spend time with her. He was too busy hoping his mother would come home.

Feeling rejected and frustrated, Angie decided to try buying small gifts for Jaylen. But even that was a dead-end street. At one point she went into Jaylen's bedroom and found all the gifts she had given him torn apart. Games were destroyed and action figures had their heads ripped off. What Jaylen wanted was his mom—not a stepmom. As loving as she was, Angela couldn't be his mother. On one occasion two years into the family, she made him a birthday cake. Jaylen said, "If my own mother can't be here on my birthday and make me a cake, I don't want one from you." It was then that his stepmom realized she couldn't fill a hole she didn't make, but she could continue offering unconditional love at a pace her stepson could accept.

Of course, not every stepparent-stepchild relationship is this dramatic or black and white, but the principle holds: pain and grief create love conflicts and affect the development of new stepfamily relationships. They affect how open kids are to stepparents and how trusting spouses are of one another.

In the largest survey of couples creating stepfamilies ever conducted, Dr. David Olson and I (Ron) found that the fear of another breakup/divorce predicted with 93 percent accuracy whether couples had a strong, vibrant marriage or a poor, unstable one. In our book *The Smart Stepfamily Marriage* we reported that fear cascades negativity on the relationship and leads spouses to be guarded and cautious with their heart. The root cause: pain from the past. It's impact: the fear of more pain. The potential outcome: to avoid being hurt again spouses do not love sacrificially or with their whole heart. This fosters insecurity within the marriage. How insidious!

You see, just below the surface in nearly every new blended family relationship is a hidden question: Do you *really* love me and can I trust you?

The antidote, however, is not to withhold your love until the other person can prove beyond a shadow of a doubt that they love you as much as you hope they do. The antidote is for you to love them with your whole heart—no matter the risk involved. It is only then that you will destroy any residual fear or apprehension you have stored up in your heart and make it more likely that the other person will move toward you in love as well.

That's what you can do about your fear. But what do you do when you see another person is fearful of loving you? Apply great patience. Have compassion for their pain. And try as best you can to love them anyway. Yes, sometimes boundaries will still have to be set with a child ("No, you can't speak to me that way"), but the key is not refusing your love even when rejected. Don't let their pain and apprehension keep you from speaking their love language.

STEPPING ON SOMEONE'S LOVE LANGUAGE

If you mispronounce a word it's hard for people to understand you. If you step on someone's love language, you violate their heart, communicate a lack of love, and hamper trust.

- A "Words of Affirmation person" can be emotionally devastated by insults and harsh words.
- A "Quality Time person" can be hurt by halfhearted or distracted listening, or by repeatedly postponing promised time together.
- A "Gifts person" can be hurt by a forgotten anniversary or birthday, or left feeling empty in a relationship void of tangible tokens of love.
- An "Acts of Service person" can be hurt by laziness, someone leaving a mess for them to clean up, or forgotten promises to help.
- For a "Physical Touch person," a slap or any kind of abuse or neglect can cause extreme emotional pain.[1]

Anyone can conduct these violations—intentionally or accidentally. When that happens, love should respond with an apology, action to make amends if appropriate, and the effort through self-discipline not to repeat the offense.

The relationship shared by insiders serves a protective function when violations occur. Insiders tend to forgive one another more quickly, give each other the benefit of the doubt, and tolerate one another's irritating personality quirks. Outsiders, on the other hand, don't get the same mercy and grace.

A harsh word from a biological parent can hurt a child, but early on a similar harsh word from a stepparent hurts the child, damages their trust, and discourages the child from wanting to move closer to the stepparent. It has multiple negative effects.

In the books *The Smart Stepmom* and *The Smart Stepdad* I (Ron) strongly urge stepparents to round off the rough edges of their personality or they may find themselves permanently outside a child's circle of trust. You cannot make a child love you, but it is your responsibility to be someone they would want to love.

This discussion begs a question: *Should you speak your stepchild's (or any other blended family member's) love language even if they aren't in a place of acceptance?* Angie bought gifts for Jaylen, but he rejected them and the message of love she was trying to convey. Should she stop giving him gifts?

Kids are interesting. Even if they are stiff-arming you, they still want to know you care for them. Angela shouldn't waste money on gifts if Jaylen is going to tear them up, but she should keep looking for "gifts" she can give him, if just to communicate her dedication to loving him. If you reject a child that is rejecting you, the message is "my love for you is conditioned on your love/openness to me." That message likely shuts the door on a possible relationship completely. No, you don't have to become a doormat. But don't give up communicating care, either.

INADVERTENTLY LOVING WITH THE "WRONG" DIALECT

This entire chapter brings us to discuss one more barrier to building love in blended families: using the "wrong" dialect. Some dialects are more intimate than others are. With the best of intentions, you can implement the love languages in an unwise dialect and have it backfire on you. We believe it is helpful to think of three levels in each of the love languages, moving from the least intimate to the most intimate. Some dialects are more intimate than others are and require a higher level of trust and openness.

Words of Affirmation

- Level 1—"I appreciate what you did for Mary. That was very kind."
- Level 2—"I can tell you really like playing soccer. I think that is great." "I like hanging out with you."
- Level 3—"I love you." "You are very important to me."

Acts of Service

- Level 1—going beyond basic daily needs (service with a smile); occasionally doing a child's chore or task with or for them
- Level 2—helping with a project the child wants to complete
- Level 3—doing something for the child that requires a great deal of time and energy on your part

Quality Time

- Level 1—"getting to know you" conversations; hanging out with a group of people; doing an activity side-by-side
- Level 2—sharing emotions; talking about positive and negative experiences

- Level 3—intimate, revealing conversations; one-on-one focused time together

Giving Gifts

- Level 1—remembering a gift that the child requested and getting it for them
- Level 2—asking the child what they would like for their birthday; giving a symbol of their value to you
- Level 3—gifts that require a significant sacrifice of time or money

Physical Touch

- Level 1—fist bump or high five
- Level 2—playing a game that involves physical touch; a side hug
- Level 3—a "bear" hug; a foot massage; a back rub

> "We haven't been married long so I'm still very careful. Her boys are still reluctant to come close to me. I'm trying to honor that."

You'll notice that the levels have aspects that are less intrusive and others that are symbolic of a deeper, more intimate relationship. It's very important that you respect these differences and not force yourself into a space where you have not been invited. If you started using Level 3 Words of Affirmation and found that it backfired, don't blame the language. You probably just didn't have the relational foundation necessary to support speaking that dialect. Your stepchild's primary love language may be Physical Touch, but that doesn't mean you can start with bear hugs. In fact, that might make them bristle and withdraw. Move gradually through these languages and dialects and trust the order above. If your efforts feel fruitless, give the slow cooker time to continue warming up the ingredient, and try again.

Let us be clear, the five love languages are fantastic tools to facilitate bonding and develop trust in blended families. Research makes it clear that among other things smart stepparents speak affirming words to stepchildren and communicate warmth for them (Words of Affirmation). They also spend time together pursuing activities or hobbies both enjoy and make time for fun (Quality Time). And they give gifts and go out of their way to perform acts of kindness that serve the child (Gifts and Acts of Service).[2] The cumulative effect is first a developing friendship that makes possible a deepening trust relationship over time. But if you move too fast, too soon in these efforts, you can make things worse.

Because blended family relationships naturally create competing loves, especially in the beginning, avoiding the barriers discussed in this chapter will help you avoid conflict and "cook" at a pace each ingredient can embrace. In chapter 5 we'll say more about implementing the Love Languages and this concept of pacing with children, but since parenting is always a function of your coupleness, we turn our attention to laying a strong foundation of love in your marriage.

YOUR TURN

Consider the relationships in your blended family.
Looking back, did you start with Level 1 actions? With good inten-
tions did you jump too quickly to Level 2 or 3? Given what you've
learned, what might you do at this point?

4

Building Love Together in Your Marriage

A COMMITTED, LOVING marriage is the first and last motivator of stepfamily integration. In slow-cooker terminology, your marriage is the electricity and heating coils that generate the warmth needed for ingredients to warm up, soften, and merge. A poor or dysfunctional marriage is the equivalent of unplugging your family slow cooker. No more heat, no more family integration.

Your couple relationship, then, is absolutely essential to the success of your entire home. So this chapter is about strengthening your coupleness. You'll learn how to communicate love to your spouse through the love languages and we'll discuss how to protect your marriage from the influence of previous relationships and blended family stress around you.

MAKING THE OTHER FEEL LOVED AND SAFE: USING THE LOVE LANGUAGES

"I struggle most with how to fulfill my husband's love language. I'm not always sure what he wants or how to make him feel important to me. I'm actually better applying my stepson's love language than I am my husband's."

Our deepest desire is to be safely loved. To experience that and have it reassured time and time again brings great joy and comfort to our souls. To offer that to the one you love is an honor and privilege—and serving them in that way, also, brings great joy and comfort. Speaking their love language significantly contributes to a safe, loving relationship.

If your spouse's primary love language is Words of Affirmation, offer a regular dose of verbal compliments and encouragement. You can tell them how much you appreciate them completing a task, caring for your children, working hard, striving to grow . . . the list is endless. Doing so requires attention and the willingness to express your appreciation directly to them verbally or in writing. Offering forgiveness is another affirmation. It makes a strong statement: You hurt or disappointed me, but I value you enough to let it go so our relationship can be restored. What a powerful message affirming their worth.

> Because his love language is Words of Affirmation, she would write him notes and hide them in his briefcase or suitcase when he traveled. Once she bought him a coffee and wrote a note on the cup. He took it to work, not realizing "Good morning hottie" was on the outside. His coworkers got a big kick out of it and the couple got a fun story they still love to tell.

If Quality Time is their love language make sure they have your focused attention when together. In other words, put down your phone and engage in attentive dialogue. Listen to their heart and respond to it. And when engaged in an activity together, which could be face-to-face (generally preferred by women) or side-by-side (preferred by men), be sure to be emotionally and mentally present.

Fundamentally, Gifts are a symbol of love. Whether big or little, handmade or store-bought, cheap or expensive, giving a gift communicates your thoughts for the person and their value to you. Give surprise gifts and predictable ones, creative gifts and expected ones. And don't forget that your best gift is you—your time, your attention, your focus, your transparency.

When you do a nice thing for your spouse, you're not just completing a task. Your Act of Service makes a statement of love and care. Sometimes this is as simple as opening a door for the other, starting their car in the winter so they can hop in a warm vehicle, or cleaning up *their* dishes. Or it might require forethought as you anticipate a need they will have at some point— say, picking up the lion's share of the household tasks while the other has to pull a lot of overtime. Whatever it is, thoughtfulness and kindness can be heard at a great distance.

And finally, the basics of Physical Touch include nonsexual touch, like holding hands, warm hugs, a gentle touch, or dancing together. Sexual touch also has a special impact on couples, serving as a reminder of their fidelity, commitment, and passion for one another. We recommend married couples have a balance of both over the course of their marriage. Together, nonsexual and sexual touch communicate that you want the other person near you and that you value who they are.

> To help your spouse speak your language, make requests, not demands. "Could you run a couple errands for me?" or "I'd love to get some time together this weekend; I'm missing our 'us' time." Clearly express your need and give your spouse a direct path to your heart.

"Where are my flowers?"

Finding clarity on your partner's love language is not always an easy road. Frequently partners have to stop being myopic about their partner and learn to love with knowledge.

In her first marriage, Cynthia and her husband both had the same love language, Giving and Receiving Gifts. Given their sameness, it was easy for them to show and perceive love. The love language of her second husband, Jeremy, is Acts of Service. Giving gifts was foreign to him. Instead, he would say, "Here's some money, honey. Go buy yourself whatever you want." For Cynthia that wasn't the same as him taking the time to go out and find something for her. Her constant disappointment confused Jeremy. He was giving her money. Wasn't that enough?

Eventually, both came to realize that they weren't loving with knowledge and they both were a bit short-sighted about their perspective of the other. For example, she had noticed all the household chores that Jeremy did around the house (Acts of Service) and to some degree realized most wives would love having a husband who did things like that without prompting, but she kept thinking to herself, "Where are my flowers?"

> When feeling unloved, manage how you respond so you don't make things worse.

Meanwhile Jeremy felt taken for granted. He put out a great deal of energy doing things for her to show his love, but she didn't see it. "She would leave her clothes on the bathroom floor and I would pick them up for her and make the bed and do all kinds of things around the house to show her that I loved her, but she didn't appreciate it."

They were caught in a classic bind. Both were expending time and energy to communicate love to the other *in their own language*—and given the expectation that the other would love them in a specific language, neither could hear how the other was attempting to say, "I love you."

Cynthia and Jeremy took the love language online assessment (5LoveLanguages.com). She discovered that his key love languages were Acts of Service and Physical Touch. Their eyes opened. Both began appreciating how the other naturally showed love and intentionally tried to speak their love language more. "I noticed all he was doing and told him 'Thank you, I appreciate that,' and he started trying to surprise me with gifts."

Discovering her dialect was very important as well. "I learned the surprise element of giving her gifts was critical," said Jeremy. Cynthia chimed in, "Yeah, it makes the gift—no matter what it is—all the more special to me." Jeremy laughed as he explained. "Right. If she finds out I've been shopping for her, I might as well take it back. It's all about the surprise."

Strengthening your insight

Hopefully by now you're beginning, if not accelerating, your ability to speak your spouse's primary and secondary love languages. The general expressions of each love language listed above will get you started (additional examples can be found at the end of this chapter). But loving your partner well in a blended family usually requires effort and insight into their particular dialect, how the past enters the present, and how your blended family adds stress on your marriage.

When you can't figure it out

Hope has been married to her second husband, Ryan, for four years and she still hasn't figured out his love language. And neither has he.

Her first marriage ended tragically when her husband Dalton was killed in a work accident. She said, "I knew his love language until the day he died, and he knew mine. We each spoke the other's language with ease." Now you know why figuring out Ryan's language was so frustrating.

"Ryan is a mystery to me. When I first met him, he said his love language was Physical Touch. But I found out he hates to be touched. He doesn't mind holding hands or kissing on the cheek, but no rubbing, no scratching, no caressing. He's okay with cuddling, but only for a short time until he gets too hot. And I have to make him hug me with both arms, not one of those weak side hugs."

In striving to understand his dialect, Hope discovered that Ryan's first marriage had affected his love language expression. His first wife didn't really care for physical affection so he shut down that part of himself to accommodate her needs. Ryan didn't completely understand what was going on either. Had his love language somehow changed?

One partner's self-awareness—or in this case, lack of awareness—obviously affects the other's ability to love them with accuracy. While you both search for clarity, don't consider the process of discovery to be a failure. If anything, the intentionality behind the search is a statement of love in and of itself. Be sure to "credit" one another's desire and effort while you listen and discern what's going on.

Then, when you do discern their particular dialect, celebrate the insight and focus your efforts in that direction. This is not to say, of course, that the other love languages are not meaningful; genuine love will express itself in all five languages over time. But when you want to make it really count, speak their primary dialect.

BLENDED FAMILY STRESS AND YOUR MARRIAGE

What gets in the way of speaking or receiving a message of love? The competing and conflicting attachments we discussed in the previous chapter will ultimately put pressure on your marriage. When biological parents feel stuck in the conflict between their child and spouse, the marriage suffers. When every response feels like the "wrong" one, discouragement can rob you of your willingness to love.

So can loyalty conflicts. One dad said, "In the beginning of our family I found myself in a no-win situation. When I spoke my kids' love language, it felt like a threat or betrayal to my new wife. I was trying to take care of them and make up for what they had been through, but it caused a lot of tension between my wife and me." The answer to this dilemma, as we discussed in the previous chapter, is twofold. Targeting their love language, the father should continue to move toward his kids while also moving toward his wife. And the stepmother should bless his connection with them, recognizing that she needs him to be a good father, so his children will be more likely to welcome her into the family. This is not an either/or situation; it is both/and.

Sometimes the stress initially centers on a stepchild's rejection or distancing of the stepparent. This is frustrating for both the stepparent and biological parent. But sometimes their ideas of how to respond differ, putting the couple at odds. One stepmom

> Commit that you
> won't let a child's closed
> heart turn you against
> each other.

wrote to us, "I'm not sure what my stepdaughter's love language is. I was loving and caring at first, but her disrespect made me pull back and guard my heart. My husband didn't like how I reacted and he defended her. All we did was fight about it." A first step in situations like this is to check your expectations. Is your eagerness to "blend" as a family and create harmony causing you to be overly anxious about the tension and cast blame? What if you recognized the child's love conflicts and relaxed your expectation that the stepparent can solve this? In the next chapter we'll give stepparents more direction on what they can do, but for now, commit that you won't let a child's closed heart turn you against one another. It may sound strange, but you can continue to love one another separate and apart from whether all the other relationships in your blended family are going well. Compartmentalizing your emotions is not always easy, but remember, your marriage is what gives others the motivation to figure out how to welcome outsiders into their heart. If you turn on each other, an unmotivated child will not become motivated to warm up to the stepparent.

Not helping children grieve their losses can also be a barrier to your marriage. Raymond had two affairs before leaving his wife and two sons. And leave he did. He saw his sons on an inconsistent basis, rarely paid child support, and quickly married a single mom. He threw himself into his new family, to the demise of his first. His sons deeply resented him for it. They had lost their father's love, their stable family home-life, their house (when their mother was forced to move in with relatives), friends, and financial stability. Then, imagine their growing sense of resentment and loss after being tossed aside by their dad for his new wife and stepson.

Loss is the elephant in the room. You have to talk about it. Don't try to circumvent sadness and demand that people warm up to others. Instead, talk about the elephant in the room. Enter the sacred places where sadness lives and share it. Children, in particular, need someone to acknowledge all they have lost, hear it objectively, and help them make sense of it. They need loving, safe guides through the journey of loss. Finding comfort in loss from the people you love and trust most is one thing that helps move children (and adults) through their loss to the place where they can take new risks and consider new relationships. And one by-product of helping one another grieve is a stronger marriage.

> Enter the sacred places where sadness lives and share it.

Before we move to the subject of stepparenting, there's one other blended family dynamic we want to talk about here that can add stress to your marriage. Couples that marry later in life and have adult children (and perhaps grandchildren) often underestimate the adjustments their children will go through when they marry or how they will react about financial matters.

"My twenty-seven-year-old stepdaughter had a fit after our wedding ceremony," said one woman. "She cried uncontrollably as we drove away on our honeymoon. My husband's son called as we left the building to report the emotional breakdown that was taking place. While he was on the phone my daughter on the other side of the church was calling to report that my husband's adult children were not helping with the cleanup because one of them was having a crying fit and the others were trying to comfort her. My husband and I looked at each other and said, 'What just happened?' We didn't know what else to do so we turned off our mobile phones and enjoyed a wonderful fun-filled romantic honeymoon that lasted five days. We returned home completely unprepared to start living the life of a blended family."

Adult children may be adults, but at times of uncertainty sometimes they are more like children than adults. Why? Because their entire world is changing—again. They feel out of control, again. They feel loyalty conflicts, again. They are losing connection and exclusive time with a parent, again. And they are losing *home*.

This is experienced in a myriad of ways. One relates to the physical home. Imagine one parent has died; going home is how they remember and experience again the parent they have lost. But imagine now, the house is sold or others are living there. It's not home anymore. We can also lose our home emotionally. Lauren Reitsema says when divorced parents remain single, kids of all ages can still identify with the pieces of their former life, but when a parent marries again the pieces evaporate.[1] This is true whether someone is five, fifteen, or thirty-five. A thirty-one-year-old daughter talked about her experience going home for Christmas, "I am now the outsider in what used to be my own family. I feel incredibly alone."

Sometimes adult kids are concerned about a parent's quick decision to marry ("I think he's going to regret this."), how it might affect someone else ("How does Mom feel about Dad getting married again?"), or what they consider to be changes to their parent's decision-making or personality ("Dad was never this energetic or warm toward Mom"). Bottom line: adult children are heavily invested in their parent and their family—and any decision by a parent to marry affects their life tremendously.

Everything you're learning in this book applies to adult stepfamilies. Grieve the past with your adult children and don't ignore their concerns about you marrying. Move toward them even as you are moving toward your new partner or spouse. Let your child, or children, and your partner build their own relationship, in their own time, and don't try to force a blend. And deal proactively with financial matters so they can rest.[2]

OVERCOMING FEAR WITH LOVE

Just below the surface in nearly every new blended family relationship is a hidden question: Do you *really* love me and can I trust you? That same question, whether originating from within your marriage or within your blended family, can exist in your marriage. What overcomes that fear is persistent, faithful love.

All too often couples wait for their fear to go away to act in loving ways. That doesn't work. Or they criticize and get angry, hoping that will make their partner act in loving ways. That, too, doesn't work. They might even retreat into the safety of their kids rather than risk loving their spouse with all their heart. That's right, you guessed it: that doesn't work either. What does work, what can move you through your fear and into the light, is doing the things that love would have you to do.

YOUR TURN

Write down any insights this chapter has given you about yourself, your marriage, and/or your family. What challenges do you face? What courage do you need to find?

MORE PRACTICAL SUGGESTIONS[3]:

If your spouse's love language is . . .

Words of Affirmation:

- Give your spouse a different compliment every day for a month. And occasionally compliment them in front of friends or family.

- Say the words "I love you" as often as you can.

- Notice your spouse's strengths and tell them why you appreciate them. Be specific: "I love the way you reach out to people who don't seem to fit."

- Text, call, or use social media to affirm your spouse or connect with them when away.

Quality Time:

- Ask your spouse for a list of five activities they would enjoy doing with you—don't assume you know. Make plans to do one a month for the next few months.

- Think of an activity they enjoy, but you don't. Tell them you are trying to broaden your horizons and would like to join them in the activity. Set a date and try it.

- Plan a weekend getaway just for the two of you. Plan your time well (e.g., grandparents with the kids, work responsibilities covered) so you can insulate your time and focus on each other.

Receiving Gifts:

- You've heard of the twelve days of Christmas. How about the twelve days of gifts for your spouse's birthday or your anniversary?

- Let nature be your guide. The next time you take a walk, keep your eye open for a stone, stick, or feather you can give as a gift. Attaching some meaning to it will enhance its value.

- Keep a "gift idea" note in your phone. Every time you hear your spouse say, "I really like that" or "I'd love to have one of those," record it. After a while you'll have a great list for Christmas, birthdays, etc.

Acts of Service:

- Do something nice for someone your spouse cares about.

- Write a note: "Today I will show my love for you by . . ." Complete the sentence with a task you know they would appreciate. (Bonus points if it's a chore that's been put off.)

- While they are out of the house, get the children to help you with some act of kindness. When your spouse returns, surprise them at the door.

- Run interference for your spouse during his or her favorite TV show or important sports event. Take care of the kids, phone calls, pizza delivery, etc. so they can really enjoy their time.

Physical Touch:

- As you walk from the car to go shopping, reach out and hold their hand.

- Walk up to your spouse and say, "Have I told you lately that I love you?" Take them into your arms and hug them while you rub their back. "You're the best."

- Initiate sex with a foot, neck, or back massage.

- Remember how you used to touch your spouse when you were first dating and begin to do that again, like you're falling in love all over again.

5

Building Love Together in Stepparenting

WHEN REFLECTING ON her journey as a stepmom one woman said, "I understand my stepkids' love language, but they don't understand mine, nor do they make any effort. I get the impression they think I don't have any feelings, but I do."

It's not always this extreme, but there are seasons where most stepparents feel that they do most of the giving and get very little in return. Stepparenting is hard. You have all of the responsibilities of caring for a child, all of the obligations and expenses, but get far fewer rewards than biological parents—especially in the beginning when everyone is trying to figure out where to put you. Biological parents don't always appreciate how hard this is, partly because even on their worst days their children forgive them and reconcile fairly easily. On most days, biological parents get a regular dose of "I love you Mom/Dad," or hugs, or smiles that communicate "I appreciate you and want you in my life." Moreover, most of this comes quickly and easily. Stepparents have to earn every reward they get.

A relationship plagued by love conflicts (loyalty issues) and a child's lower motivation toward love and bonding are usually at the roots of this. Get past those challenges and stepparents find many rewards (along with all the regular angst of parenting children that biological parents experience).

One significant predictor of blended family satisfaction, for both adults and children, is whether the stepparent can find a workable role in the home. While each person contributes to the process, finding your place, defining your role, and establishing yourself as a trustworthy parent-figure are keys to building love.

LEAD WITH LOVE. LISTEN FOR LOVE.

In chapter 4, we saw how Jeremy and Cynthia figured out each other's love language. While on that journey, they also had to figure out how to build love with their stepchildren. Each brought children to the marriage. Jeremy had three kids, two boys and the oldest, a girl; Cynthia had two sons.

"I had been single for ten years before Cynthia came into our lives," Jeremy said. "Through her teen years my daughter, Chloe, had been the only woman in our home. If we bought towels or something, she picked the color because she was the woman of the house. When Cynthia came into the picture, she had her own opinions of decorating the home, what foods we should eat, and lots of other things. As you can imagine, Chloe felt displaced. They really butted heads."

> It's hard to move toward someone who continually moves away from you.

Cynthia chimed in. "It has been really hard for me to show her love when she is distant all of the time, even now as an adult. Through the years she would get close to me a little, but then feel disloyal to her mother and move far away. That hot and cold response from her has made it hard to keep showing her love. So at this point, I try to show her love by loving her daughter, my granddaughter."

Cynthia is leading with love and finding whatever avenue she can to express her love (in this case, through her granddaughter). It's hard to move toward someone who continually moves away from you. But successful stepparents persistently lead with love. They are wise in how they do so, but they don't give up. Your sacrifice precedes a child's increasing motivation to love. When your efforts are reciprocated, by all means, enjoy every minute of it. But when they aren't, ease off on the intensity of your efforts (we'll say more about this later in the chapter), but keep looking for a way to express yourself.

It might help you to keep persevering if you step into your child's shoes and consider why they might keep their distance. Chloe was the "princess" of the home before the new "queen" dethroned her. It's hard for parents sometimes to understand just how important roles like this are to children. In her case, contributing to the home and providing leadership to her younger siblings held value for Chloe. She lost that when Cynthia entered the home. Not only did Chloe then have to compete with Cynthia for the time and energy of her father, she found herself wrestling to hold her value.

Shifts in birth order have similar effects on children. A child who is the oldest in one home is a lost middle child in the other. Or a fun-loving baby-of-the-family who gets lots of attention at her father's house is nearly invisible with Mom and stepdad who have newborn twins. Changes like these affect a child's self-esteem and add more loss to an ongoing narrative of loss and unwanted transition. No wonder Chloe couldn't readily receive Cynthia into her heart. So what is Cynthia to do? Continue, with wisdom, to gently and persistently lead with love.

A second reason Chloe remained distant was a love-conflict. All things being equal, stepparents should assume that children will first and foremost remain loyal to their biological parents (whether living or deceased). Moving closer to Cynthia, on occasion, made Chloe feel guilty, as if she was abandoning her mother for a relationship with Cynthia. Protecting their parent and preventing conflict takes a lot of emotional energy for a child—and requires constant vigilance. This can be emotionally taxing for a child.

Though sometimes confused by it, Cynthia found a way to deal with Chloe's "hot and cold" responses. She continued to lead with loving actions, though she did so at a pace Chloe could receive (more on this later in the chapter). Sometimes it's helpful to speak directly to a child's fear. "Chloe, I want you to know that I really care for you and am glad you're in my life. And I'm honored to be playing a small role in your life. But please know, that I know, that your mother is very important to you—as she should be. I will never try to take her place. She is your mom and I will respect her as such." The goal in making a statement like this is to alleviate Chloe's fear that Cynthia is competing with her mother. If she can relax and not worry about that, she might let herself move toward Cynthia a little more.

Incidentally, we would also encourage Cynthia to communicate this same message directly to Chloe's mother. If her anxiety about Cynthia's role in Chloe's life decreases, she will relax towards Cynthia, which will in turn help Chloe relax even more.[1]

Cynthia's husband, Jeremy, had his own journey with her

sons. Jeremy and his stepson David had a hard relationship. They had started out well enough, when David was only eight, but things went south when David became a teenager (this is not uncommon). They struggled for years. You may remember from a previous chapter that Jeremy's love language is Acts of Service and he assumed early in the marriage that this was, also, the best way to show love to his wife. He made the same incorrect assumption with his stepsons. "I tried to show David love by doing things for him. I'd fix his truck, clean up his dishes, and pick up his messes. But he would never show appreciation for any of it." At least that's what Jeremy initially thought.

> "Adult stepchildren are difficult to get to know, and I've found it hard to learn their love language due to distance and everyone's schedules."

The findings from the 5LoveLanguages.com assessment gave Jeremy some key insights about David. He discovered that David's love language is Words of Affirmation. That turned on a light for him in two ways. First, instead of just doing nice things for David he began giving him compliments and speaking encouraging words to him. It was then he realized that David had noticed his efforts all along. "He might not say it to me, but he would brag to others on the things I did for him," Jeremy said. "When introducing me to his friends he would say things like 'This is my stepdad, Jeremy, and he fixes my truck for me.'"

What do you know? David did notice. And he appreciated it.

Cynthia jumped in. "David won't directly tell Jeremy he loves him. He's never said that. But he will say nice things about him. Realizing this has been huge for both of us."

Cynthia had a similar experience with both of Jeremy's sons, James and Andrew. Both boys' primary love language is Quality Time. James would seek out Cynthia at parties, even if his biological mother was there. "But he still won't say the words, 'I love you,'" she added. "For whatever reason, he just can't say it, but he will spend time with me and talk to me." Andrew couldn't tell her that he loved her either. "But he does spend a lot of time talking to me about stuff. He will ask my opinion about things and he, too, will sit by me and talk even when his mom and stepdad are in the room."

This reveals an important point for stepparents: in addition to leading with love, be sure to listen for love in the native language of each child. Notice that three of Cynthia and Jeremy's five children would never say the words "I love you" to their stepparent, but they all communicated love in their own way. You might be missing your stepchild's indirect expressions of love because you're only listening with your ears. Learn to listen with your eyes (notice their acts of service), your watch (when they spend quality time with you), arms (physical touch), or your hands (gifts), but mostly with your heart. Learn to appreciate what they can say—no matter how they say it. Loyalty concerns and sadness for missing family members may dictate that they not express their appreciation or love directly (out loud). Be wise enough to decipher the indirect message and take it to heart.

Leading with love and listening for love helps you find and establish your place in the home. But you also have to define your role and establish yourself as a trustworthy parent-figure.

THE FIVE P'S OF STEPPARENTING

Partner with your spouse.

Partnering is about strengthening your coupleness so you can love and lead your children well together. You need to partner in two ways.

First, you need a strong marriage. A solid, reliable relationship is what fuels both partners' ability to do the work of parenting and in the case of the stepparent, empowers them to be part of the authority team. Parenting is hard work; it takes a lot out of us. And—have you noticed?—until children mature it's often a one-way street. We do all the giving and they do all the taking! What spurs us to invest so much of ourselves in our children is, for many, a relationship with the Divine (who continuously pours love into our hearts), and a healthy marriage. Said another way, investing in each other ensures continued investment in your stepchildren.

To do this well, both of you need to shift your primary life allegiance to your spouse and fully commit yourself "till death do you part." Permanence and dedication contribute to an emotionally safe environment for both adults and children. Making this shift can be difficult for some parents. Before a first marriage "leaving" your father and mother to establish a new home is one thing, but "leaving" your children (that is, shifting your primary allegiance to your spouse) is another. But you must make the shift or everyone—you, your children, and your spouse—will walk on eggshells wondering what stressor might sever your marital bond. A stepparent simply cannot find their footing in the home if the biological parent doesn't elevate their status in the eyes of the children. You must have a strong marriage.

Please hear us: this does not mean you neglect your kids! It simply means repositioning them in your heart so your long-range loyalty belongs to your spouse. Couples in first marriages raising their biological children don't neglect their kids either, but their marriage does serve as the foundation to the home—and yours should, too.

Secondly, you must partner around your roles in parenting and play to each other's strengths. Ron's wife, Nan, has taught school for nearly two decades. She has served as an administrator, full-time teacher, and on occasions has been a substitute teacher. For good reason she prefers not to be a substitute. I bet you can guess why. Do you remember having substitute teachers in school? Play day! Everyone knew subs felt out of place, didn't know the routine, and occasionally could be manipulated. However, the same students who would give a substitute a hard time respond with respect to the full-time class teacher. Why? Because she has a clearly defined role and relationship with the students but a sub doesn't.

Biological parents have a clearly defined role and relationship with their children. On day one, stepparents have neither. They are substitute parents. And without the biological parent's support and backing, they may have a disruptive classroom experience. Which brings us to the subject of child behavior management.

People sometimes confuse discipline and punishment. Discipline is about training a child. It's about building their character and teaching them the ethics of life. Punishment is about correction and consequence. It is a negative form of discipline. Stepparents can on day one in the family slow-cooker offer discipline to a child, but should punish sparingly until a clear bond and trust is established.

When biological parents take the lead on handing down punishment to a child, they are playing to their strength and partnering with the stepparent by not putting them in a tough situation. When they communicate to their children that the stepparent "is in charge while I'm gone," they are giving the sub a chance to be successful. And when they gently insist that their teenager act respectful ("Don't talk to my husband that way."), they are giving the substitute parent a chance to be viewed as an authority in the home.

Stepparents partner with the biological parent when they consult with them before making rule changes or modifying family traditions. And they are playing to their strengths when they don't expect too much of themselves. For example, assuming you can fill all the "gaps" in a child's life may be well intentioned, but is unrealistic. One stepmom decided she would change the diet that her husband and boys were used to; they were going to "eat healthy" if it killed her. It almost killed her place in the family. Until your relationship status is set, work with your spouse and move slowly on making changes.

Over time, stepparents can clarify their relationship with stepchildren and gain tremendous influence and authority in their life. You may start out as a substitute teacher, but following the five P's won't leave you there. In most cases, as your relationship deepens with a child, so will your role in their life.

STEPPARENT MISSTEPS:

- Being overly harsh on stepkids or your spouse's parenting. Be very careful how you offer criticism, even if you think it is constructive. Begin your observations with, "Because I care about Tim . . ."

- Demanding love and affection or terms of endearment ("Call me Mom.")

- Viewing the time your spouse spends with their child as a threat to you. A balance of time and energy between you and your stepchildren helps move you into the family.

BIOLOGICAL PARENT MISSTEPS:

- Becoming paralyzed in your parenting. Due to guilt over the past, fear for your child's future, or sadness regarding what is happening in your home, some parents become paralyzed in setting boundaries or following through with discipline. Resist this temptation.

- Holding on to "veto" power. Don't hinder your spouse's influence or involvement in parenting just because these are "your kids." Make space for the stepparent.

- Not trusting the stepparent's heart toward your child. You may not agree with every aspect of how the stepparent relates to your child, but guard against judging them as uncaring. That sets you against them and teaches your children not to respect them.

Pursue

If you want to make a new friend you have to extend yourself in their direction—and you must do so in ways that make it more likely they will open themselves to you, and perhaps, pursue you back. Smart stepparents continually pursue the liking of their stepchildren. Be fun and warm. Smile at them. Spend time doing things they enjoy. If you aren't approachable, don't be surprised if they don't want to hang out.

Pursue Tips:

- Take an interest in their interests and share your talents, skills, and interests. Find common ground.

- Share your desire to get along. "I really want to get to know you."

- Be their biggest cheerleader in life. Applaud their efforts and show confidence in them.

- Be careful with comments like "My kids never acted like this" or, "Your daughter is very irresponsible." Your spouse might become defensive and guarded.

- Make sure children know you're not trying to replace their mom or dad. In fact, go out of your way to support their relationship with the parent in the other home or the memory of a deceased parent.

- A good way to enter their life is to keep up with their daily activities. Take them to soccer practice, ask them about their math test, and play with them.

- Match the child's level of openness to you. If they are uncomfortable being with you one-on-one, orchestrate group activities so someone else is involved. Move toward one-on-one activities when you can.

- Be sensitive to a child's experience of loss. Show compassion for their grief, allow them to talk about losses, and encourage ongoing connection to parents and extended family not in your home. Compassion is attractive.

- The average stepfamily needs five to seven years to integrate their family and bond relationships. Be patient with the process.

Of course, one of the best ways of pursuing a child is to know and speak their primary and secondary love language. Cynthia and Jeremy utilized the online profile (5lovelanguages.com). Some abbreviated profiles are included in chapter 2. In addition, we've provided a summary of principles to help you discover your child's love language at the end of this chapter.

If your stepchildren are adults, keep in mind your initial goal is being *friendly*, not necessarily openly "loving." If we gave you the assignment of making friends with a new neighbor, you probably wouldn't introduce yourself and immediately give them a bear hug and kiss on the cheek (unless that is a common cultural greeting). Make friendliness your initial goal. That will likely be more palatable for them.

No matter a child's age, it could be that both of you are just now learning about the love languages. But it could also be that the biological parent knows their child's love language and the stepparent is just now exploring this. The biological parent has much to share, but both of you should know that the upheavals of the past may have created traumatic experiences for a child that have altered or even soured their love language.

Noah's love language was Quality Time. He and his dad used to spend hours together hiking and fishing. But ever since the divorce, his dad rarely spends time with him. And when he does show up for visitation he is on his phone with work or his latest girlfriend. Now, when his dad says he's coming by, Noah would rather not see him. But neither can Noah spend lots of time with his stepdad, who is more than eager to speak his love language. Guilt, love conflicts, and hurt have soured Noah's receptivity to quality time.

It could be that Noah's mother is able to speak the language of Quality Time to him while his stepfather can't, at least not yet. He should continue to pursue Noah, but may have to take the love language "path of least resistance" we discussed in chapter 3. Start with the least intimate, least potentially intrusive dialects of each love language—Giving Gifts, Acts of Service, and Words of Affirmation—and move toward the most intimate—Quality Time and Physical Touch.

Both parent and stepparent are seeking to understand a child's primary love language so most of the time you can speak what communicates best, but you should utilize all five over time. Everyone needs love spoken in a variety of ways. Moreover, you don't want to speak just one exclusively. This is especially true of gifts; only giving gifts may cause them to see the world through materialistic eyes.

Now here's the catch for stepparents. Pursuing makes you vulnerable; it hands power over to a child, especially one who is closed toward you. The least invested person in any relationship always has the most power. This is another reason to partner with your spouse who can shut down any manipulation.

In addition, don't let your pursuit turn you into a pushover. You can still say "No" and risk disappointing the child; in fact if you don't they may never respect you. Rather, walk the line of deepening your friendship and trust in one another while remaining the adult in charge.

As if all this weren't complicated enough, you need to consider your biological child's feelings as you reach out to your stepkid. One stepdad asked, "How do you balance giving gifts to a stepchild in front of your own child, whose love language isn't Gifts, but still sees the other child receive something from me?" The answer is to continue loving each child as best he can. Not everything has to be equal (in gift giving, for example) but it should be fairly equitable (meaning, generally similar). And he may offer an explanation to his child. "I could buy you a gift, too, but I also know what you really value is spending time with me. Let's find some time this weekend, just the two of us."

Pace

A child's "pace" should inform a stepparent's pursuit of their heart. Gauge a child's level of openness to you and match it.

Throughout this book we've offered a number of cautions to stepparents about not demanding love or pushing themselves onto a stepchild. But the principle of pace trumps all of that. If a child has thrown herself wide open to you, disregard the general precautions and go for it! However, matching their level of openness also means backing off if they are closed or uncertain of how to receive you. Sometimes it's not personal at all; their visitation schedule or life situation can determine how much time you are together. You have to make the most of what they give you and the opportunities you have and trust that time will multiply the impact.

Patience

Blended family complexity means patience is a must. "My stepson and I can find a good rhythm together in giving and receiving love—until he goes to his mom's house for a few days. After that, he's different with me for a while and we have to regroup." This is a common experience for stepparents. Patience in that season is a must.

You can also be patient with yourself. "In the beginning I felt so overwhelmed. I had to step back and take a breather every once in a while, and then I felt like I could give again without feeling resentful that my stepkids weren't speaking my love language." This form of self-care is wise, but be sure to explain to your spouse what you're doing so they don't resent you pulling back a little.

> Eagerness trips up many well-intentioned stepparents.

Ironically, eagerness trips up many well-intentioned stepparents. It sets you up to give without limits and expect it to be appreciated. Many "wicked stepmothers" are really just overly eager caregivers who are trying to make everything right for a child who has been through many painful experiences. Repairing the child's life and being desperate for the child's love and acceptance make many stepmoms appear to be overbearing and emotionally fragile.

There are many moving parts in a stepfamily and the depth of a child's heart has many layers—most of which you don't control as a stepparent. Cut yourself a break and perhaps lower your expectations of how quickly you can bond and how thoroughly you can intervene in their life. This will help you not tie your success or failure as a stepparent to how open they are to you and may give you some thick skin to endure tough moments. In the end, patience will move you through times of uncertainty and take some of the pressure off the loyalty conflicts of children.

Persistence

The ups and downs of stepparenting can be discouraging. And for many, the temptation is to emotionally withdraw to sulk or punish, to get angry, to retreat into your own children, or to just give up. Well, we'd rather you be stubborn. Stubbornly persistent, that is, in gently pursuing (while pacing with) the child.

You can't be a bull in a china closet. Just be determined to keep pressing forward. No, you don't have to constantly set yourself up for disappointment with a child who is completely closed to you. But neither should you give up and walk away. If their door is completely shut, knock occasionally. And if nothing else, stand outside and when you can speak to them through the door, all the while continuing to live your life on your side of the door.

Sometimes the door is open to you, but you have to persist for a very different reason. In total, John and Kerri had three kids in their blended family. His youngest is a Physical Touch child. "Always in someone's lap," Kerri commented. Her son and his older daughter both respond best to Quality Time. "Without it," John said, "my daughter will become a funky, moody teenager. We've learned to stay on top of that or things get bad." The problem is, John's kids spend most of their time at their mother's house where they receive very little Touch or Time from their mom or stepdad. "At their house, kids are expected to occupy themselves and if they ask for some attention, in effect, they are told to 'go away,'" John lamented. "If anything, they are told what they are doing wrong and that's about it. We sort of have to make up for that with extra cuddle time and conversation when they come to our house on Friday nights. We have to make the most of our time with them."

Kerri's stepchildren were hesitant to receive love from her when they weren't getting it from their biological mom. But Kerri doesn't mind persisting for their sake. She knows loving them well ministers to their soul. "When you love your kids well, it makes it easier for them to carry that love with them to the other home. We can't make their mom love them better, but we can fill them up before we send them over there."

"And here's the biggest surprise," said John. "We've even noticed this has changed my ex-wife's attitude toward co-parenting with us. We used to have a toxic relationship with her. It was ugly. But we made a decision a year ago that regardless of what came at us we were going to love her however we could. And the easiest way to do that is to love my kids well so when they leave here their cup is full. And what we've noticed is that when they come back it doesn't take as long for them to acclimate to our home, but it's even made a difference with their mom. She feels our respect and kindness through the kids and it's making a difference in how she responds to us. She called me recently—usually she is angry about something—but she didn't complain about anything or criticize us; she just wanted to coordinate our calendars. I couldn't believe how considerate she was," he said. "This is happening more and more and is a big change for us. Even more importantly, it helps my kids out a lot because they don't get caught in the anger and crossfire."

Did you catch that? No matter their age, loving your kids well fills their cup and helps them cope with life in the other home—and might just help change the attitude of your co-parent toward you.

The bonus "P"

There's one more "P" you might consider. Prayer. As parent and stepparent you need to constantly bathe the process of parenting in prayer. The principles we've given you provide a basic road map, but you need God's wisdom to know when to zig or zag, when to keep going, and when to back up and start again. Prayer will keep you humble and listening. Praying *together* will keep your hearts connected and unified.

If after reading this chapter you realize mistakes have been made, regroup as a couple. Talk about what you've learned and decide how to proceed. Apologies may need to be made.[2] You may need to recalibrate your roles, expectations, and efforts going forward. You may need to strive to heal specific relationships—maybe even the entire family. Prayerfully develop your plan together and be patient with yourselves as you step into the future.

YOUR TURN

How are you doing with the five principles of healthy stepparenting? Which are strengths right now and which need improvement?

HOW TO DISCOVER YOUR CHILD'S LOVE LANGUAGE[3]

For both parents and stepparents there are a few developmental considerations to keep in mind when trying to discover your child's primary love language and preferred dialect. Speak all five love languages to children under the age of five, especially to infants who need lots of physical touch for healthy brain development. As your child grows you'll notice a pattern in how they express love to you and others. You'll also notice one language spoken by you communicates your love more deeply than the others and when spoken negatively results in more hurt. This awareness will help you pinpoint your child's primary love language.

One caution: don't discuss your search with kids in the preadolescent or teen years or it may tempt them to manipulate you. A Gifts child may beg you for the latest smartphone or an Acts of Service child may "forget" to clean their room to take advantage of your willingness to serve. Maintaining proper boundaries and expecting your child to pull their own weight are acts of love, too.

LOOK FOR THE PATTERN: TIPS FOR FINDING YOUR CHILD'S PRIMARY LOVE LANGUAGE

Considered together the following indicators will help you identify a dominant pattern in your child. Consider them collectively.

Watch how your child speaks love to you. All kids want to give and receive hugs or gifts, for example, but what language do they repeatedly speak? Young children especially (ages five to ten) are likely to speak the language they desire most to receive. Do they compliment you or thank you for helping them with something (Words of Affirmation) or ask to spend time with you (Quality Time)? Do they repeatedly give hugs or sit in your lap (Physical Touch)? Watch and learn.

Observe how they express love to others. Expressions of love to teachers, grandparents, and extended family members also indicate a child's preferred love language.

Listen to what your child requests or complains about most often. "Mom, how did I do?" or "How do I look in this?" are bids for affirming words. Likewise, what a child complains about may fit their overall pattern. "Why are you always looking at your phone, Dad?" is a request for focused time.

Give your child a choice between two options. "Would you rather go shoot hoops together or get your mom a special gift?" "I have some extra time this evening. Would you rather we take Gracie to the dog park or I help you study?" Over time, the preferences to these kinds of questions can help you see a distinct pattern in your child.

Remember, the pattern that emerges for each child with the biological parent or stepparent may vary. It's okay if you are focusing your efforts on different love languages because the child's receptivity is key to the message getting through.

6

Building Love Together in Sibling Relationships

WE HAVE A THEORY about sibling relationships in blended families. Whether they are a half-sibling (sharing one biological parent) or a stepsibling, if you took them out of their family circumstances and introduced them to one another, some of those who don't get along in their blended family, would hit it off and fare pretty well, maybe even most. Of course, at school, church, or in a neighborhood not all children get along; there are many reasons kids don't become friends. But for half- and stepsiblings, the larger blended family dynamic has great influence on sibling relationships. If the family as a whole is doing well, half-siblings and stepsiblings have a better chance of becoming "siblings" in more than name only. If the family is struggling, at least some of the sibling relationships will struggle, too.

THE TIME FACTOR

One estimate is that two-thirds of kids in stepfamilies have either a half- or stepsibling relationship.[1] Just over 12 percent of all children live in a household with a stepsibling, half-sibling, or other unrelated "sibling" (that is, not adopted or biologically related).[2]

How much time half- and stepsiblings spend with one another and whether they think of one another as family influences how close they are. Half- and full siblings share a parent, perhaps even a last name and family history, and they have more communication and contact with one another over time so they tend to have more well-defined bonds than stepsiblings do. Half-siblings who live together all or most of the time generally think of themselves as brothers and sisters. They function more like siblings, too (they identify as family, care for each other, socialize together, and support each other emotionally). However, when half-siblings have little contact, they tend not to view one another as siblings or act as such.

Time together makes a big difference for stepsiblings, as well. Generally speaking, stepsiblings are less close than half- or full siblings, but not necessarily negative toward one another. They just tend not to think of one another as brother or sister unless they have lived together over a long period of time. Further, stepsiblings who enter one another's lives in the first few years of life and have consistent family time together can feel very connected and often maintain a strong relationship into adulthood.[3] Some stepsiblings immediately connect because they have longed for a sibling ("I've got a sister!") or share a common interest ("We both love fantasy football!") while others want little to do with one another for a host of reasons.

WHAT GETS IN THE WAY

Time and age aren't the only issues impacting sibling relationships. In this chapter we share practical ways you can create a climate that will help siblings of every age build love in your blended family. But before we do that, let's explore some of the barriers that stand in the way for both adult and minor-aged children.

Remaining strangers

Of course, some stepsiblings and half-siblings spend a great deal of time together because they live together either full- or part-time. But some never meet, or have limited exposure to one another. Siblings of all ages may live in different parts of the country and rarely interact due to a host of reasons. We're running into more and more people, for example, who were never told about their half-siblings but learned of them as adults. For those who do know one another, busyness can stand in the way. Adult stepsiblings may have full and active lives with children of their own, careers to manage, and various other commitments that squeeze out time with stepsiblings.

Not having much in common

It's hard to make friends with someone when you have little in common. Likewise, it's hard for stepsiblings or half-siblings to enjoy one another's company or want to be around each other if they don't like the same things. It's even worse if they like opposing things. Divergent opinions about social and political issues, religion, financial priorities, even movie preferences can naturally pit siblings against one another. And then there's sports.

For three generations Daniel's family (including his kids) were North Carolina basketball fans. He met and married Emily, who graduated from Duke University. And so did her brother and parents. Emily's kids had been raised to worship Coach K, while Daniel's children wore Carolina blue every chance they could. Do you smell a rivalry? March Madness became a metaphor for this family's merger madness!

Differences like this usually result in a friendly competition that eventually becomes part of the family story ("Boy, we used to argue about who was the best"). But for a season (pun intended) it can divide a family quickly. Be sure to model attitudes that keep rivalries like this friendly, and don't let them get personal. When the competition is over, teach children how to disagree without being disagreeable and model loving "your enemy."

Clashing personalities

We've all known people who simply rubbed us the wrong way—someone who talks too much, someone we think is pushy, someone with odd quirks, someone who's just plain selfish. These people are difficult to be around whether at work, school, or in family relationships. They can bring out the worst in us. When sibling personalities clash, parents can speak to both sides: moderating your quirks to not annoy others and the value of loving others despite our differences. You may not want to hang around them in your free time, but you do need to see them as individuals created by God with worth and value. We can love people even if they annoy us. Love is choosing to treat them with respect—as we would want to be treated.

Rivalry

Full, half-, and stepsiblings have multiple reasons to compete for parental time and energy. Resist the temptation to try to talk kids out of their emotions ("You don't need to worry about how much time I spend with your stepbrother"). Instead look for opportunities to validate their concern and see the desire hiding underneath their behavior. "When you pick on your stepbrother, does that mean you wish you had more time with me?" If the answer is yes, then look for opportunities to meet that need. Then you can suggest something like, "The next time you want us to do something together, just tell me rather than picking on Jack. Okay?" The following dynamics contribute to sibling rivalry. Be aware and sensitive to these concerns in children.

Birth order changes. For many children, one of the significant changes that comes with a parent's marriage is the presence of older or younger siblings who, in effect, alter the child's birth order. This can spark a rivalry between stepsiblings. For example, an oldest daughter becomes a "middle child." Throughout her life she has enjoyed the rights and responsibilities of being the oldest sibling—a role that helped the family survive the single-parent years—but now she is not needed, not the leader. Given that birth order is part of our identity, a child who experiences a significant shift in sibling order may take out their angst on the sibling who has replaced them.

When there's less to go around. It used to be common for American families to have many children. If you had six brothers and sisters, for example, you expected to get hand-me-down clothes, to struggle for one-on-one time with your mother or father, to receive fewer birthday presents than other kids at school. But at the end of the day, your siblings were your family, too, and most likely you understood why parental time, energy, and money were in short supply.

However, when your parent marries and instantly your family doubles in size (and then grows again if more children are born into the family later), you might resent having to share a bedroom with a stepsibling, competing for time with your biological parent, and how financial resources now have to be distributed. This can hamper new sibling relationships, especially if it feels like someone is getting special treatment.

Sensitivity to "unfairness." Both adults and children are more sensitive to differences in how other children are treated by adults in stepfamilies than in biological families.[4] For example, a stepmother may, at the same moment, feel threatened by the special "princess" pampering her husband gives his biological daughter and envious that her daughter doesn't receive the same treatment from him. The stepsisters may well notice it, too.

These feelings can arise in biological families, too, but the sensitivity around this issue is much more pronounced in stepfamilies.[5] Therefore, if you want to reduce the rivalry between half- and stepsiblings, it is important for biological and stepparents alike to avoid showing preferential treatment to one child over others.

Joy was a classic "favorite child." Her mother named her Joy because she was her "pride and joy." Joy was the first "ours" baby added to the "yours" and "mine" family of children brought into the marriage. Her mom let everyone know she was her favorite. As a result, Joy's siblings treated her like the biblical character Joseph's brothers treated him for being his father's favorite. They resented her, and, like Jacob's household, the favoritism sparked division in the family.

It's okay to have special connection points with each of your kids, but favoring one above the others is unjust and problematic. Check your motives, love them all, and be equitable in how you treat them.

Competing attachments and insider coalitions. One stepmom, Jasmine, noticed that her children and stepchildren found it difficult to be around each other, in part, she concluded, because she got more time with her stepchildren who lived with her full-time than with her own kids who lived with their father part-time. Adding insult to injury, two of her children's primary love language was Quality Time. "They get you all the time and we just get you half the time. But they don't even want you." They were right. Of course, Jasmine felt guilty about this, but there wasn't anything she could do about the circumstances. But she could be intentional in how she loved both sets of children.

> "We've been good about establishing new traditions in our family. But one of my daughters has struggled to let go of the old traditions because it means letting go of her mom—and she wants more of her, not less. This has kept her a bit disconnected from the other kids in our family."

You might remember that in chapter 3 we talked about competing attachment triangles and how parents can move toward both sides to help reduce the competition between them. Remember that each side of the triangle—in Jasmine's case, her children and stepchildren—are hoping to move toward her so she must give them some of herself in order to reassure them that she cares and is still there for them. That reassurance is a prerequisite to either side softening regarding the "competition."

This process gets even more difficult to accomplish if a group of insiders have formed a coalition against an outsider. If a subgroup of siblings, for example, have decided to mistreat a stepsibling, it will take direct intervention from you to break the coalition and insist on appropriate behavior. "You don't have to like one another, but you are going to be decent to each other or you will feel some consequences from me."

Conflict with a stepparent impedes stepsibling relationship. When a stepparent and stepchild are having a difficult time connecting or getting along, out of loyalty the stepparent's child may not get along with the stepsibling. "I don't like how you're treating my dad, so forget about being my friend." It is only when the stepparent and stepchild improve their relationship that this dynamic will begin to change.

Pseudo-connection. Sometimes stepsiblings have less conflict than full or half-siblings, but the reason for it may not be as positive as it sounds. When stepsiblings have a pseudo-connection, that is, when they don't know each other well or feel like family, ironically they have less negative interaction and more positive communication. They act, like most of us do with strangers, on their best behavior. However, feeling securely connected to a sibling frees people to be more honest with negative emotions and different opinions. Now here's what's interesting about this: the more bonded stepsiblings grow over time, the more conflict you can expect.[6] Terrific. Just . . . terrific.

Awkward attraction

Though rare, sometimes stepsiblings don't get along because one or both of them are secretly romantically attracted to one another. Conflict is a defense mechanism to avoid an awkward crush. Stepsibling romance does occur. In the book *The Smart Stepfamily* Ron discusses at length why stepsibling attraction happens and what you can do to guard against inappropriate touch in your home.[7] Online he has addressed what parents can do if stepsibling attraction has already occurred.[8] That discussion is beyond the scope of this book. But we do want to raise your awareness about this subject and caution you. Due to the easy accessibility of online pornography we believe the incidence of stepsibling romance and sexual curiosity will rise in the years to come. Viewing porn—or being exposed to it through a friend—confuses family boundaries and either opens a child's heart to entertain the idea, invites conflict into the relationship to make sure it doesn't happen—or invites both. In any case, don't stick your head in the sand. Establish common-sense boundaries in your home that respect one another's privacy, guard against porn exposure, and talk candidly with your children about related topics. Your family needs your guidance and protective concern.

REALITY CHECK

You can't force relationships between stepsiblings any more than a stepparent can demand love and acceptance from a stepchild. Yes, there are things you can do. But it's important to first acknowledge what you cannot change. Adult children who have busy lives and who don't define a stepsibling as a brother or sister probably won't prioritize time with them. A child who feels betrayed by a decision you made in the past (say, an affair that ended your first family), likely won't open themselves to a relationship with a half- or stepsibling that came about because of your betrayal. Sincere apologies and forgiveness lead to reconciliation. This opens the door to better sibling relationships.

Stubborn children with opposing viewpoints or personalities will find friendship challenging. In these and other circumstances, you need to lower your expectations and relish small victories, be-

> You may need to focus most of your attention on relationships that are going well or are open to your influence.

cause there is so much you can't change. Choosing your battles carefully and not pushing your agenda at every turn are helpful strategies, as well. Further, to avoid constant disappointment, you may need to focus most of your attention on relationships that are going well or are open to your influence, while applying the Pace principle (see chapter 5) to those that aren't. And always, no matter what, strengthen your marriage. Creating a climate that encourages connection between stepsiblings always starts there.

CREATING A CLIMATE OF CONNECTION

Strengthen your marriage

Dan and Jen's two oldest children (ages fifteen and fourteen respectively) knew each other at church. His son, Jacob, told her daughter, Katherine, that he thought his dad had a "thing" for her mom. And he was right. Katherine went and told her mom what Jacob had said, and Jen came right out and asked Dan if that was correct. Despite being taken aback by the question, Dan admitted his feelings for her, and they started dating.

Most couples meet and start dating before their children are aware of what's happening. But even if they brought you together in the first place, you still have to strengthen your marriage over time, for it acts like gravity in your family: it draws all things to it.[9]

Do you recall earlier we said that your marriage is the first and last motivator of bonding in your home? The permanence and health of your marriage gently invites stepsiblings and half-siblings alike to find a way to get along. If siblings can't find any other reason to open their hearts to one another, your marriage means siblings and extended family aren't going away so they might as well figure out how to adapt to the circumstances. Said another way, necessity is the mother of motivation. The resulting boost in motivation just might be what it takes for siblings to move beyond the status quo and toward a closer relationship. So continue to invest in and nurture your marriage relationship despite what is happening between your children.

Apply love language wisdom

Because all of us need to feel loved, talking about the five love languages and encouraging each family member to take the love language quiz can be the road to building better relationships. When each family member knows the others' primary love language, they have the information they need to express love in the most meaningful way.

As parents, we help our children understand that learning to speak the love language of other people will be an asset to them in all future relationships. Our family gives us an opportunity to learn how to speak love languages that may not be natural for us. Our goal is to learn how to speak all five love languages. Keeping this concept on the "front burner" in family conversations can be fun, and will create a positive emotional climate in the home.

Seek to build bridges

If someone is struggling with a steprelationship, you can always use what's happening to try to build a bridge. For example, to an older teen or young adult who spends less time in your home compared to their younger siblings and stepsiblings, a stepparent might say, "Maybe you feel a little awkward, as I do, about how much more time I'm spending with the other kids than you these days. I'm still trying to figure out all of this myself. I want to spend more time with you, but that just doesn't seem likely given your time at college. And it feels like this issue is making it tough for you and my kids to get along. I'm not sure I'm seeing that correctly, but it feels that way. I really want to respect your feelings, so, may I ask how you're feeling about all this? What would feel right to you at this point?"

By the way, this is what we might call a DTR conversation—that is, Define the Relationship. You may have heard DTR applied to dating relationships, but bringing definition and shared expectations to any ambiguous relationship helps everyone involved know what is expected of him or her and others. This takes some anxiety out of the situation and helps people settle into the relationship.

Have fun and gather around common ground

In chapter 5, we encouraged stepparents to begin forming a relationship with stepchildren by capitalizing on what you have in common. In the same way, orchestrate activities for stepchildren that you know they both (all) like. Having fun, side-by-side, or making memories together doing things everyone enjoys are good first steps—and always gives kids something to return to if all else fails. Just be careful not to force uncomfortable levels of participation. Remember to be aware of their level of openness and trust that they will warm up and soften as time goes on.

Expect the golden rule

Actively hold your kids accountable for "doing to others what you would have them do to you." Expect them to be kind to one another, fair, and considerate of each other. Notice, there is a clear distinction here: you are not expecting familial type love or affection, but you are asking them to treat one another in the manner they would like to be treated. Showing consideration, for example, invites children to put away selfishness and consider another's welfare. And when personalities clash or viewpoints differ this teaches kids to disagree without being disagreeable. Over time, this helps create a family culture of "warmth" between stepsiblings.

Recognize the importance of each child

When there is rivalry over limited parental time and attention, make sure you call out the unique value of each child no matter how much time they have with you in the home. This sends a message to stepsiblings that everyone is valued and important by you, and invites them to celebrate the uniqueness of their stepsiblings also.

If one of your children responds to you with jealousy or anger about a stepsibling, recognize the need this reveals in your child. They want to know they aren't losing you to their stepsibling and need to be reassured. Calmly explain what you see happening and help the child identify their emotions and behavior. Over time this raises a child's emotional IQ and helps them manage their own emotions. "Hey bud, I've noticed when I say something nice about Sara you get quiet. Are you feeling invisible to me? I do still see you—and love you so much. You're not any less special to me. [Pause. Let the child respond if they are willing.] Now that you know you're still important to me, you should know that I will still give Sara compliments from time to time. Maybe you can too one day."

Encourage cheering for each other

When possible, encourage stepsiblings to attend one another's concerts, athletic games, competitions, and activities so they can cheer for each other. Encouraging someone helps you root for them on and off the court. Celebrate accomplishments as a family.

Create rituals of connection and tradition

Family traditions are things we do, generally during holidays or special days, that tell us who we are and who we belong to. Celebrating someone's birthday with a special tradition communicates love, value, and the importance of the person—it enhances and gives meaning to the birthday celebration. In the beginning, blended families don't have "family traditions." Some family members have shared traditions and others don't. That's why forming your own traditions over time is so important. It helps bring definition to the family and draws people into the importance of the moment.

Putting a new spin on an old wedding tradition can be a helpful strategy here. Something old, something new, something borrowed, something—well, let's forget blue. Try to honor some old traditions while you discover what will define you in the future. You may have to try and fail a few times, but in creating traditions strive to keep something old, make something new, and borrow from each other till you find what works.

Rituals of connection are regular, sometimes daily behaviors that family members do that connect us. Giving your spouse a kiss at the end of a workday is a ritual of connection. Saying goodnight to your kids by tucking them in bed is another. Help stepsiblings create these connections, but let them define how it is done and when. Young children may give hugs and kisses before bedtime or going to school, but teens may need to avoid physical rituals altogether (for reasons we discussed earlier in this chapter) and instead find a verbal cue to greet or say goodbye to one another. The point is this: rituals of connection over time add to the warmth of the family blend. Encourage them when you can.

Road trip!

Have you ever noticed that strangers who go through foxhole experiences bond in extraordinary ways? Soldiers who serve together become lifelong friends and everyday people who survive a natural disaster or auto accident together stay connected long after. A "radical road trip," a strategy recommended to stepparents in *The Smart Stepfamily* (Ron Deal), can also be used to help stepsiblings form bonds.

Ordinary road trips include driving to Grandma's house. But *radical* road trips might involve going on a family mission trip to another part of the country or world that requires you to stick together, work hard side by side, and perhaps brave unfamiliar territory. In addition to doing good for others, conditions like these can break down barriers, give family members a new perspective about one another, build memories everyone will love to tell over and over, and in the process, forge relationships between stepfamily members.

Is there a selfish agenda in this act of selflessness? A little. But it may just be what your family needs to move past the status quo. And, if you take an annual radical road trip, you build a new family tradition that builds character in kids and gives meaning and mission to your home.

"Out of respect for me . . . "

We believe that some of the strategies in this chapter will improve stepsibling relationships in general over time. But what if they don't? What if one of your children refuses, for whatever reason, to be kind or decent, or give others a chance? If all else fails, a biological parent can appeal to their child directly to "act better than you feel out of your love for me." If they won't be kind for the sake of their stepsibling, maybe they'll do it for your sake. One father told his son, "You don't have to love them, but they matter to me and this family. So out of respect for me, please be decent to them. If nothing else, treat them like you would a coworker or neighbor." His appeal gave his son just enough motivation to make a few small changes. Everything helps.

AND FINALLY: FIND CONTENTMENT

Of course, it is your hope that the children of your blended family will eventually love one another and consider each other family. Some will naturally move in that direction, others will be friendly but not friends, and still others for whatever reason will not connect much at all. Strive to create a climate where friendliness can lead to friendship, which can lead to "familyness," but don't make that a requirement of your joy. Too many couples consider their family a failure if all the siblings aren't comfortable with each other. That just makes it difficult for you to enjoy your marriage (that is healthy) or the sibling relationships that are working well. Being content with what is going well is not the same as giving up on what isn't.

YOUR TURN

What are you doing to "warm" the sibling relationships in your blended family? What needs improvement?

Building Love Together in Grandparenting

TIANA'S FACE LIT UP with a smile from ear to ear. "You're right, she doesn't leave her daughter with just anyone. I never thought about it like that. This is so helpful."

Tiana is stepmom to Aniyah and stepgrandmother to Hannah. Her relationship with Hannah is fantastic; her relationship with her stepdaughter, the granddaughter's mother, not so much. At least, so she thought.

After listening to Tiana describe her adult stepdaughter's distance, I (Ron) made an observation she had never considered. "Aniyah drops her daughter off with you fairly regularly, right? She may not need a close relationship with you, but she doesn't mind you having one with her daughter. Don't miss the message embedded in that. Parents don't just drop their kids off with anyone, so she must trust you to care for her daughter. That is an indirect reflection of how she values you. She might not be able to communicate that to you directly at this point, but it certainly is being said. On some level she trusts you. No, it's not the same as her loving you, but since trust is often a precursor to love, it seems to me you have more going with her than you realized." Tiana had never thought of it that way. She was encouraged.

Stepgrandparenting involves three generations of family members, and each person involved has needs, desires, and a stake in all the other relationships. Thus, this chapter explores these relationships from multiple perspectives, offering something for each generation. We suggest you share it with the other generations (depending on the age of children, of course). Reading and then discussing it may help all three generations understand how they can better love the others.

BLENDED FAMILIES: TALL AND WIDE

The new marriage of a blended family is part of either the older generation (we'll call it the *upper* generation) or the *middle* generation (adult children). Families of European descent often only think of the household with stepchildren in it as "the stepfamily"; in reality, the blended family includes at least three generations and multiple households. In some situations there are former in-laws, who are still invested grandparents, making the family system even broader. We like to say blended families are tall *and* wide.

Stepgrandparenting is common in the US today. Nearly 40 percent of all families in the US include a stepgrandparent,[1] and by 2030 it will be almost as common for grandparents to have a stepgrandchild as a biological grandchild.[2] And while we don't have much research to draw from to understand what makes for healthy or unhealthy stepgrandparent relationships, two dynamics stand out: bonding in all three generations is always determined by the least invested person, and middle-generation adult parents serve as the gatekeepers for stepgrandparents.

In chapter 5, we observed that the least invested person in

any relationship has the most power over the level of closeness in the relationship. That's true in a business relationship, dating relationship, marriage, in stepparenting, and in stepgrandparenting. If a stepgrandchild doesn't care to let you into their life, you won't be able to build a strong bond. If a stepgrandparent doesn't desire closeness with an adult stepchild or stepgrandchild, it simply won't happen until their heart opens. And a middle-generation parent can prevent their child from having a close relationship with the stepgrandparent. This *gatekeeping* behavior dramatically impacts the role the older generation can play.

One stepgrandmother who married into a family in her older years went to the hospital to support her stepdaughter who had a baby. After spending a couple of days in the waiting room with other family members, the woman noticed two things: the family thanked her for coming (none of the other grandparents were thanked; as full-fledged family members it was assumed they would be there, but not her), and she didn't get to hold the baby nearly as much as the biological grandparents. Why? Because the baby's parents (middle generation) limited her time with the newborn.

Who is the least invested person in your situation? Are the gatekeepers opening the gate or keeping it shut—and if so, why are they moderating the closeness between generations? (If you were to ask them, their answer may differ from yours.)

We hope in this chapter to help each of you understand the other's experience and needs as it relates to grandparenting. We encourage you to consider the other's needs above your own as you seek pathways to mutual respect and varying degrees of connection.

"I THOUGHT THEY WOULD BE FINE WITH ME
GETTING MARRIED AGAIN ... "

When the middle generation is the one that made a decision to marry and form a blended family, they tend to be highly motivated to figure out the role of the stepgrandparent in the lives of their children. But when it is the upper generation that has made the decision to marry, adult children, just like younger children, have a wide variety of emotional responses. This can blindside later-life couples. "We just didn't see this coming," one man in his late sixties said. "It's been many years since their mother died and my children expressed concern that I would feel lonely. One of my kids even encouraged me to date online. I thought they would be fine with me getting married again, but they haven't been." His wife then added, "I thought adult children should be adult about this."

While adult children should monitor their contributions to family stress, upper-generation couples should not judge adult children too quickly and recognize the many adjustments a wedding requires of them—and the many losses it brings. Further, they need to respect their children's concerns so they can move toward those concerns and not make things worse.

So what's going on with the middle generation?

"It Feels Like We're Losing Her All Over Again"

Loss is a fundamental story line in the backstory of every blended family. How that loss occurred also affects how an adult child responds to their parent's later-life marriage. Divorce, for example, cuts short a child's family narrative and stability (no matter whether the child was young or an adult when the divorce occurred), but how the divorce came down also matters.

A parent who has an affair, repeatedly lies to their spouse and children, abruptly abandons everyone, leaving them to fend for themselves financially and physically, and runs off to Cabo with their new lover should not expect a warm response to a wedding announcement. Your actions have caused great pain. Your "gain" has brought great loss to your kids. That matters. Not every example is this extreme; still the point remains: the backstory to a new marriage matters and you must adjust your expectations of adult children accordingly.

> Loss is a fundamental story line in the backstory of every blended family.

There is a different story from the middle generation after a parent dies. It goes something like this: "Mom and Dad had a good marriage. It wasn't perfect, but they loved each other—at least we thought they did. When Mom got cancer we fought it together. Dad took care of her . . . he did everything right. She's only been gone a few months. How in the world did he move on so fast? Did he ever really love Mom? It feels like we're losing her all over again."

In a situation like this, the data points just don't line up. Dad's decisions are confusing his adult children, leaving them questioning everything they know—or thought they knew—and doubting their dad. To readily support his marriage to another woman—not to mention bless her role as stepgrandmother—is at best going to take some time.

That's one takeaway for upper-generation couples: you might need to slow your roll toward the wedding. And once married you certainly need to maintain reasonable expectations for how quickly family members will embrace one another. All of the love conflicts, dynamics of competing attachments, and varying motivations toward accepting each other as family that have been discussed in this book still apply to adult children. It doesn't matter that they are "adults." Loss is loss. Change is change. Be sensitive to all of this and remember, the backstory matters.

"The Outsider in My Own Family"

What we as parents of adult children (both of us, Gary and Ron, have adult children) often underestimate is the psychological significance of our role in their lives. We represent "home."

In relation to our parents we all view ourselves as the child. Maybe you, like we, have encountered the strange experience of caring for aging parents. Isn't that upside down? They're supposed to care for themselves and us—we don't make decisions for them! Life feels disordered when we have to care for an aging parent. And to cope, we all must adjust our expectations and redefine our identity as it relates to the other.

In a similar way, children of divorce sometimes find themselves providing for their parent emotionally and carrying more responsibility in the home. Later, when a parent marries, adult children again find themselves having to adjust to their parent's changing life. Whether it's fair or not, we want stability in our parent's lives so they can support us in our somewhat unpredictable and occasionally chaotic lives. My adult life may be a mess, but I can always "go home" to find stability. To find love. To be cared for.

A parent's marriage sends ripples through the generations. One significant change for adult children is the sense that they can't "go home" anymore. It's just not the same. One adult daughter said, "When I go to my mom's house for Thanksgiving there are many people there from her husband's family that I don't know—his children and grandchildren, and extended family. I am now the outsider in what used to be my own family. I feel incredibly alone."

Stability is lost, it's harder to be cared for, and you have to compete with strangers for the time, energy, and attention of your parent. But for some it's even deeper than that. Feeling alone at home is about their very identity. You may remember from chapter 5 that when a parent marries the splintered pieces of a child's original family—and their place in it—fracture even further. Not only is it not home anymore for the adult child, they are having to reestablish their place in the family and in the world. If my identity is tied to my family and the family changes, who am I?

Ron once talked with an adult brother and sister, Ryan and Samantha, about perceived competing attachments that were keeping them from embracing their dad's new wife and her family. Their parents had divorced after over thirty years of marriage. The siblings had families of their own at that point and had to help their children deal with the fallout. A couple years later their father married a woman with children and grandchildren. Before they knew it, the special name their children had created to refer to their grandfather, "Paw Paw," had been adopted by his new stepgrandchildren. Ryan and Samantha and their entire side of the family felt displaced and were angry their dad let himself be called that. The message Ryan and Samantha feared their kids would receive was, "You aren't special, but my new family is."

Is that the message their father intended to communicate? Probably not. Was it fair for them to accuse him of not caring for them or their children? Objectively, one could argue for either side, but that's not the point. Family disruption and subsequent transitions erode family stability and shake the foundations of our identity and perceived value in the family.

We believe there's emotional work to be done on either side of this equation. Upper generation couples need empathy for how life-disrupting a wedding might be for adult children and should move toward those grown kids with patience, words of affirmation, and other expressions of love to help ward off their crisis of identity. And, middle-generation adults may need to deal emotionally with their perceived losses and further establish their sense of identity separate and apart from their parents' relational choices. Neither is easy, but both are necessary.

Seeking Value: Money and Estate Concerns

Loss of identity is not the only thing that can make an adult child feel devalued in the stepfamily mix. Loss of money—that is, poorly managed matters concerning family inheritance—communicates the same message.

When more money is consistently spent by a parent on their biological children than on their stepchildren, the stepchildren and their parent are likely to perceive that they are less valued. A blended family spouse whose partner constantly lets their ex dictate how their kids' medical bills get paid will also feel less valued. When someone after marriage refuses to revisit the beneficiary list on their life insurance, their new spouse may feel suspicious and anxious that they "rank below children" or even a former spouse in the family.

Likewise, after a parent marries, adult children may have questions about the family inheritance (including cash, assets, and items of sentimental value). How those questions are answered and the attitude of both parent and stepparent toward the discussion can significantly influence if and to what degree a stepgrandparent is received into the family—and whether the gatekeepers allow them access to grandchildren.

We tell later-life couples that many times questions like "Whose name is on the life insurance?" or "Are you still putting aside college money for our kids like you did before you got six new stepgrandchildren?" are first and foremost about value. On the surface they are asking about money, but more critically, below the surface they are asking if they are still important to you. Family transitions (especially unwanted transitions) seem to call that into question. Always answer the value question first. "Because you kids matter so much to me, I want to keep you informed about what is changing in my financial situation and what is staying the same. Ultimately, what I want you to know is that my wife and I are making sure all of you are provided for. We are creating a trust that will take care of everything should something happen to me. Let me tell you the details . . ." Always affirm someone's importance before answering above-the-surface questions.* Then, deal with the practicalities of money and inheritance in a straightforward manner (and put your plans in writing). Adult children have a right to know what's going on and may need to speak into the process. Try to consider one another's needs as you do so.

Resurrected Wounds

For some adult children there's one more thing going on behind the scenes that is affecting how they respond to a stepgrand-

---

* By the way, even after doing so, you still need good answers to blended family money questions. A full discussion of this topic is beyond the scope of this book, but Ron and colleagues Greg Pettys and David Edwards have created a comprehensive guide in their book *The Smart Stepfamily Guide to Financial Planning* (Bethany House, 2019). It examines both above- and below-the-surface aspects of managing money in stepfamilies.

parent and whether they open the gate or keep it closed. Old first-family wounds can easily be resurrected when a parent's new love creates a new family.

"You never loved Dad this way." Jason was confronting his mother about her announced engagement. "You gave Dad second-best and it crushed him and ruined our family. And now you want me to be happy for you?" Clearly, Jason was still hurt over his mom's decisions. He had forgiven her—and he thought he had worked through his anger. But seeing his mother love another man with her whole heart resurrected his pain because, for the first time, he could see what his parents' marriage could have been like.

> Old first-family wounds can easily be resurrected when a parent's new love creates a new family.

When wounds rise once again to the surface, both generations need to recognize it for what it is and process the hurt—separately and together—in order to find a path forward. The challenge here is bridging the emotional gap between the generations. Earlier we discussed what happens when the new couple, which is eager to move forward with their relationship, and adult children, who are again struggling with pain, overlook the others' needs; a Grand Canyon can quickly form between them. The grandparent and new partner quip, "What's wrong with those selfish kids?" and the adult child feels forgotten and invalidated.

Because loss must be grieved afresh over time, resurrected pain is an opportunity for parent and child to move toward each other, not with blame, but with apology, forgiveness, and reconciliation. Don't miss your opportunity, every time it arises (we recommend Gary's book *When Sorry Isn't Enough: Making Things Right with Those You Love*).

Avoid a quick turnaround

Further complicating relationships between upper and middle generations is what we might call a "quick turnaround" marriage.

After forty-two years of marriage, Greg's wife passed away when he was sixty-six. After forty years of marriage Paula (age sixty-five) became a widow. Both spouses died in May. Greg and Paula connected online in September, met face-to-face for the first time in January, told their adult children they were seriously dating in March, and announced plans to marry in May, one year after becoming widowed.

This is what you call a quick turnaround.

When he heard the wedding announcement, Greg's middle son said, "Gee, Dad, Mom's dead, but not that dead." And when Greg asked his oldest son what kind of special plans he should make for their wedding night, his son responded with just one word. "Gross."

Baffled, Paula's children talked about what they should do. "Mom has always been very frugal with her money and careful with relationships, but she seems to have thrown all of that out the window. I want nothing more than for her to be happy, but she's not in the driver's seat." "Yeah, she's spending money and making decisions I think she'll regret later. We need to talk to her about this."

Upper-generation adults need to recognize that quick turn-arounds add doubt to an already stressful adjustment for middle-generation adult children—and ultimately adds another barrier to stepgrandparenting. If adult children don't trust how the relationship was formed or the permanency of it, they may be even more guarded with their children.

By the way, we are not suggesting that later-life couples wait for approval from their middle-generation children before getting married. But unwise is the couple that blindly runs into marriage without recognizing the negative impact of ignoring their children's feelings. Your children care for you, are wrestling with their own adjustments, losses, and identity issues, and are deeply invested in your life decisions, so move toward marriage at a pace that considers them (Ron's book *Dating and the Single Parent* examines this thoroughly).

> Unwise is the couple that blindly runs into marriage without recognizing the negative impact of ignoring their children's feelings.

Which of the above dynamics are part of your family dynamic? If you are sharing this chapter with the different generations, share your observations, try to empathize with one another, and discuss how you move forward.

HOW DID YOU ENTER THE FAMILY?

In addition to adjustments related to the middle generation, the quality of grandparent relationships in a blended family is affected by how you entered the family. Said another way, what type of stepgrandparent are you?

Earlier in the chapter we referenced a situation that could be called *later-life stepgrandparenting.*[4] This occurs when someone later in life marries a grandparent and they acquire adult (or near-adult) stepchildren and stepgrandchildren. Usually the older adult is highly motivated to connect with all three generations. Whether that is reciprocated depends. If adult children refer to their stepparent as "my dad's wife" and don't define themselves as a "stepchild" (or their children as "grandchildren"), it probably won't be. However, if the middle generation comes to value the stepgrandparent, then connecting across the generations becomes possible.

If the middle generation is nearing adulthood and their lifestage does not afford the later-life stepgrandparent an opportunity to be involved in their parenting, the older adult is what has been referred to as a *skip-generation stepgrandparent.*[5] They may not become close with the adult child, but they have an advantage as stepgrandparents: when stepgrandchildren come along, they cannot recall a time when the older adult was not in their life. This makes bonding with the stepgrandkids more likely and can indirectly encourage acceptance by the middle generation. Still, the middle generation has to make up its own mind and will influence the level of closeness between the other two generations.

When a child who has had a stepparent for many years becomes an adult and has a child of their own, their stepparent becomes a stepgrandparent. The quality of the relationship between the *long-term stepgrandparent* and their now adult child influences the amount of time with the new addition to the family and the quality of the relationship. But because the child has always had the stepgrandparent in their life and likely was able to bond with them while very young, their relationship can supersede the relationship between their parent and their stepmom or stepdad. In fact, we've seen situations where the relationship between stepgrandchildren and the stepgrandparent helped bring healing to a stressful relationship between the upper two generations. The heart of middle-generation parents, who witness their child being loved well by a stepgrandparent, can be softened.

One becomes an *inherited stepgrandparent* when a grown biological child becomes a stepparent. Notice that in this situation, the older adult did not make a conscious decision to move into this role. In the other three types, the stepgrandparent at some point "walked in" to the situation while inherited stepgrandparents got "tossed in." Thus, these stepgrandparents may have to grow into their motivation to build a strong, close relationship with stepgrandchildren. Further, they may experience love (loyalty) conflicts between investing in their biological grandchildren and their newly acquired stepgrandkids.

As you can see, each situation has natural advantages and disadvantages, which affect stepgrandparenting and generational relationships. What can you do to address these factors and those affecting the middle generation?

BRIDGING THE GENERATIONS

Because grandparenting in blended families is a three-generation endeavor, each generation has its part in strengthening the family. Key words for everyone include patience, pace, and pursue. As much as it depends on you, find ways to live in peace and improve your relationships.

Stepgrandparents

One universal tool stepgrandparents have available is engagement. The more engaged you are, the more influence and opportunity you have. Yes, as previously discussed, you cannot make someone receive your love or love you. So you must move at their pace, but your willingness to engage is your power. And, of course, the five love languages serve as a guidepost to how you engage. The wisdom outlined in the previous chapters on pursuing relationships and the best order to apply the love languages are relevant to both your developing relationships with adult stepchildren and stepgrandchildren (see chapter 5).

If barriers stand in your way, talk with your spouse and perhaps those involved and try to understand their viewpoint. If the middle generation, for example, is distant, engage with your stepgrandchildren in ways that honor the pace of both them and their parents.

It's helpful to articulate to adult stepchildren that you recognize that you are not their parent—nor will you try to replace their parent. Not being a threat to their biological parent relationships is an important boundary to clarify. Also, be willing from time to time to step back and let them have exclusive time with your spouse and other family members. Giving them the gift of Quality Time with those they cherish reflects well on you.

Another boundary to define has to do with family identity and terms. Ambiguity in steprelationships adds to feeling disconnected. Try bringing clarity to the current state of your relationships by having a conversation around what to call one another, both in private (in your home, for example) and in public. A later-life stepmother and stepgrandmother might bring it up to an adult stepchild this way: "Normally a stepparent like me might refer to someone like you as 'my child' or 'stepchild.' And you might introduce me in public as your 'stepmom.' But I'm wondering what feels comfortable to you in our situation. You're twenty-eight years old; I'm certainly not trying to be a mother to you in any way. Actually, you might be more comfortable introducing me as your 'dad's wife.' What feels best to you? And how would you like me to refer to you?"

What you are getting at here is a mutually agreeable definition of who you are to one another and what is, therefore, expected of your relationship. This helps clarify the ambiguity and gives you both a path to moving forward. By the way, the terms you use for one another might change over time as a reflection of your deepening care for one another. Or not. Nevertheless, it's important for you both to agree on those terms.

And finally, inherited stepgrandparents who are conflicted about their child's decision about marriage can be tempted to be overly critical of his or her parenting or family circumstances. These won't make right what you feel is wrong. Instead of erecting more barriers for the family, strive to bring positivity and hopefulness to the situation.

Grandparents

Be on everyone's side. Demonstrate an attitude of inclusiveness within the generations, but don't force ingredients to "cook" on your timing. Rather, be patient as you move toward acceptance of the stepgrandparent (see chapter 1).

Move toward your children with time and energy, and move toward their grief. You are a vital part of their family story and they need to know you still share their story—and what you've lost together—even though you're now married. Moving toward them in this way eventually helps them move toward your spouse.

Proactively communicate with your children about inheritance and financial matters, especially in later-life stepgrandparenting situations. The middle generation needs to know that they and their children are still being considered. *The Smart Stepfamily*

Guide to Financial Planning is a highly useful resource addressing blended family finances and long-term planning.

And finally, staying connected with biological grandchildren who primarily live with your child's former spouse can be difficult, especially if the divorce was contentious and you feel stuck between them. It's tempting in these situations to avoid spending time with your grandchildren, which makes it nearly impossible for the stepgrandparent (your spouse) to engage with them at all. Talk with your child and explain that you are not being disloyal to them, then continue to pursue time with your grandkids.

Adult Children

Take responsibility for your emotions, resentments, hurts, and fears. You must seek resolution of these concerns; don't sit and wait on your parent.

At the same time, acknowledge that your parent has legitimate needs and desires that may have resulted in a new relationship. It may be awkward and take time, but choose to make room for new family members and extend the hand of friendship to them. Build bridges, not walls.

And lastly, even if you're struggling, don't stop your children from loving your stepparent just because you can't. Their relationship can stand on its own.

Holiday preparation

Finally, when it comes to holidays and special days, proactively discuss your expectations about who will be there, when they will arrive, what people need to bring, and what is expected of them. For example, each set of grandparents can decide how much they will spend on child birthdays and Christmas gifts, but stepgrandparents should expect to spend relatively the same on stepgrandchildren and biological grandchildren. There should be no favoritism.

Also, find creative ways of dividing time. Many stepfamilies have three, four, or more sets of grandparents. Finding time for each of them to share in special days can be challenging. Communicate your hopes, negotiate turns and opportunities, and occasionally take a backseat so someone else can have a turn. In the long run, a sacrifice here and there will likely pay good dividends. As we like to say, grace connects, but possessiveness divides.

THE POWER OF GRANDPARENTS

Grandparents are often deeply cherished in families. Grandparent-grandchild bonds can be second only to parent-child bonds, making grandparents important assets to families, especially during times of family instability and stress. In other words, grandparents matter. And so do stepgrandparents. Striving for love and maturing relationships between the generations is a vital part of growing a healthy blended family.

YOUR TURN

Which of the dynamics in this chapter affect your family?
Take a minute to list them and then decide who else you could
discuss them with. Consider how to move forward
in light of these current dynamics.

8

Building Love Together in the Face of Rejection

"What I've found as a stepdad is that it's a lot easier for me to love him if I know he loves me back. Sometimes you feel like you're beating your head against a wall. And when you're not getting anywhere, you just feel like giving up."

IN ANY RELATIONSHIP, a positive response from the other person, any sign that suggests they too are invested in the relationship, encourages your heart. And in blended families, it encourages you to continue trusting the slow blending. But what if you get nothing in return—or worse, you are told you aren't welcome?

Rejection happens. And if it is happening to you, it hurts. It may help if you understand why rejection happens and what you can do about it. That is the focus of this chapter.

By the way, we're not talking about the typical uncertainty of bonding new steprelationships. One mistake some stepparents make, for example, is to perceive hesitation from a child as rejection. This should be expected as motivations to love vary (see chapter 1). Or stepparents can misinterpret an older teen or young adult child's seeming disinterest as resistance to the new family.

Chances are that son or daughter is preoccupied with growing up, launching their life, or raising their own family.

Those are predictable, normal stepfamily "growing pains." In this chapter we're talking about the hurt you feel when a child or extended family member adamantly refuses to let you in.

Rejection can make you want to give up.

When you are highly motivated toward building love, rejection is terribly discouraging and defeating. And, as the stepfather said above, it can make you want to give up. As you'll see, what is needed instead is a persistent, stubborn, patient love.

BEHIND REJECTION: THE PAST

Elizabeth's two children were by two different fathers. The father of her first child isn't engaged in the life of their daughter, but the second father has a close relationship with her son. "Given that my daughter has never really had a dad in her life, you would think she would be thrilled with my husband entering the picture. But what she really wants is her biological dad. So my husband has been shut out. My son is open to him, but my daughter isn't."

The specific stories behind rejection vary, but when you dig underneath the surface, a handful of themes emerge again and again. These core narratives can greatly affect someone's willingness or motivation to love, and therefore, your ability to build love together in your blended family. Some have to do with what's happening in your family's present, while others have to do with the past. We have already mentioned many of these themes in earlier chapters, but will call them to your attention here.

Trauma and Loss

Elizabeth's daughter is not open to her stepfather in part because of loss. It's hard to welcome a new person into your heart (stepdad) when what you really want is someone who remains unreachable (her biological dad).

Vanessa felt rejected by her adult stepchildren *and* her husband. Benjamin had lost his first wife, Michelle, to cancer after thirty-two happy years. She died just two months after being diagnosed. He and Michelle had a close family, cherished their children and grandchildren, and were heavily involved in their lives almost on a daily basis. Grief drove Benjamin to pressure Vanessa to join him in the daily routine he and Michelle had created with their children and grandchildren and value it as much as he and Michelle had. Vanessa did enjoy their company but did not always want to center their social life around his family. She wanted to be her own person; she resisted being pushed into Michelle's mold. Benjamin's loss—not only of his wife, but their family rhythm—had led him to try to repair the family by making Vanessa function like her predecessor had. When she did not fulfill his expectation, his disappointment led him to withdraw from her emotionally.

Varying definitions of love

What a stepparent calls loving and what a stepchild calls loving can be two different things. Given this gap, a stepchild might perceive themselves as being respectful and loving toward the stepparent (as in the "love your neighbor and pray for those who persecute you" kind of love), but the stepparent still perceives it as rejection because they can't get as much access to the child's heart as they desire.

Competing attachments

Holding tightly to an established relationship might mean being partially closed to a new one. The person doesn't want to jeopardize what is to them the most significant relationship, so they show one relationship preference, even to the detriment of the other.

We should add that sometimes what looks like a love conflict really is a statement of the importance of both relationships. Many times throughout our counseling careers we have heard a child say to a stepparent something to the effect of "I like you—that's my problem." To like or love the stepparent feels like being disloyal to a biological parent (whether the parent is pressuring for loyalty or not). This conflict can result in rejection-like behavior (though it really isn't rejection at all).

Hurt

What often shows itself as anger, depression, emotional distance, or an uncooperative attitude is really hurt. A child who feels hurt by a parent's actions that led to a divorce can then feel rejection toward whomever that parent marries. Resolving the hurt and seeking forgiveness are crucial to healing and then building love in the blended family.

Confusion

A child in the midst of the physical changes of puberty and adolescence, figuring out their identity and coming to terms with the ending of their original family can be even more confused by the formation of a stepfamily. Who do I love . . . and how? Who am I to you? What is expected of me? Who am I safe with? Who do I belong to and what is my family narrative now that the characters have changed? There are a great many questions that can cloud a child's openness toward outsiders.

BEHIND REJECTION: THE PRESENT

Pain from the past gets in the way of loving in the present. In addition, issues in the present should be considered when trying to make sense of rejection.

Personality, cultural, and religious differences

It's hard to be friends, let alone family, with someone who has vastly different interests or core beliefs about life. Two strong, first-born personalities can clash as they debate the issues—all while trying to emotionally connect. Stepfamily members with different socio-political perspectives might find it terribly difficult to get along. A stepmom who believes only in eating healthy foods may find her "Taco Bell" clan turning up their noses at everything she prepares.

Families from different cultures, ethnicities, or even regions have more to merge than other stepfamilies. When "casual California" meets "formal deep-South" or "urban bustle" meets "sleepy suburb," people must overcome their differences, stereotypes, and assumptions or they may remain unable to connect.

> Religious differences can be harder to deal with because they are tied to a sense of truth about God, the universe, and our place in it.

However, differences in personality and culture can be overcome in time as people come to understand one another. Religious differences can be harder to deal with because they are tied to a sense of truth about God, the world, and our place in it. Many interreligious families have deeply held convictions that they are not willing to change, especially when it comes to their children. Parents (including a former spouse) are very invested in what their children are being taught; discussions about religious values are tantamount to fighting for the soul of their child. This may be contributing to a sense of rejection in the home.

Couple breakups before marriage are not uncommon when religious differences are vast. You cannot walk in two polar-opposite directions together. This is why we strongly encourage unmarried couples to reconsider trying to do so. If this reality did not hit home until after you married and you find yourself already in an interfaith marriage, we suggest that you strive to find shared space in what your faiths have in common. Acknowledge the differences with children (if appropriate to their age) and teach them how you intend to share what you have in common and live in the gap. Practically this is challenging and to some degree perpetuates an "us and them" divide in your home, but hopefully not one that results in rejection. To foster respect for the other's beliefs, occasionally join them in religious practices or activities that are acceptable to you. And finally, repeatedly talking and teaching children your values will also mean repeated conversations about loving each other despite religious differences. Likely this is not an issue that will go away, so be prepared for the long haul.

Your contribution to the strain

It's important that you recognize your part, however inadvertent, of the strained relationship. For example, in chapter 5 we examined how not respecting a child's pace in receiving you (or bonding with you) usually makes connecting more difficult. Distancing from a child adds to the child's justification for rejecting you. One stepdad found it easy to connect with his stepdaughters, but his thirty-three-year-old stepson wouldn't even acknowledge him when in the same room together. "He doesn't recognize my existence," he said, "so I ignore him, too. I know it's not right, but this is how I deal with it." His reaction is unfortunate. Not only is it "not right" but it contributes to the emotional distance. Situations like this often devolve into a mutual blame game. Can't you just hear the adult stepson telling someone that his "horrible stepdad won't show him any consideration, while the stepdad is telling his friends that his stepson "won't acknowledge his existence"? However this mutual cold war started, you've got to take responsibility for your side of the interaction and give the rejecting person a reason to give you a chance, not more reason to discard you.

You've earned rejection

Whether because of a harsh parenting style or a destructive habit like porn or substance addiction or simply being untrustworthy, you may have earned your rejection. If so, stop what you're doing, apologize, and change your ways! Depending on how much hurt you've caused and how long this has been going on, forgiveness and healing may take a while—perhaps a long while. But start the process by humbling yourself, owning your actions, making appropriate changes, and begin to live out of respect and love even if the other person seems completely closed toward you. Don't expect healing to occur quickly, but start the process as soon as possible.[1]

Marginalization and alienation

When someone is contributing to another person being distant or partially closed toward you, they are marginalizing you; when one person is actively engaging in psychological manipulation to prevent someone else from having any relationship with you, they are alienating you.

Nicole is a stepmom. At times she feels encouraged about her relationships with her stepchildren of four years; at other times, she doesn't. "The kids' mother doesn't help. She tells them, right in front of me, that I don't care about them. She checks them out of school when it's our custody time without communicating to us about it and calls them continually to interrupt our time when they are at our house. We try not to retaliate, but it's tempting sometimes."

Behavior like this does contribute to marginalization of the stepparent. It also makes children little pawns in the war between adults. If we had one strong word for parents it would be, "Please do not do this to your children! You might think you are guaranteeing that you don't lose your kids to the other home or a stepparent, but mostly you are selfishly making your children responsible for your insecurities."

By the way, Nicole doesn't have to be a passive victim of this treatment. She may feel powerless at times, but she and her husband, Tim, can take measured and appropriate action. For example, if the mother says something negative in her presence she can step out of the kids hearing and gently, but assertively say, "You know that isn't true. I do care for them. Please stop putting the kids in the middle. I know you'd never want to hurt them, but it does." Remaining calm is the single most important factor in situations like this, otherwise, you give the other person just cause to see you as worthy of their criticism. Once they have private time with the kids, Nicole and Tim can also say something direct to the children without criticizing their mother. A curious and gracious tone is helpful. "I'm not sure why your mom said Nicole doesn't care for you. We do love you very much. (Hug.) And if you ever wonder about this, you can just ask us."

Alienation is an extreme form of marginalization and usually results from the intentional effort of one parent to separate emotionally and psychologically the children from the parent(s) in the other household. One mother shared that for many years her ex-husband had been telling their son things like, "We like you better" and "They really don't want you at their house, but we do." "Now," she said, "my son is picking up their propaganda and beginning to repeat those words to me when he says he won't be coming over for our time. We don't know what to do." In another situation, a mother systematically implanted memories in her child in order to build a wall between the child and his father. "Do you remember when your father didn't come to pick you up at your game? I had to take you to their house. You remember that, don't you?" The mom had arranged with her former husband to take the child to their house, but then made up a story to make the dad look uncaring and dismissive.

On his *FamilyLife Blended* podcast, Ron interviewed Helen Wheeler, a therapist and parent coordinator who specializes in high-conflict divorce and cases of parent alienation. She shared that it is counterintuitive for a parent to go out of their way to hurt their own child in order to make life difficult for the other parent, but still some do. They put their child in a psychological rock-and-a-hard-place, which results in anxiety, depression, confusion, anger, and frustration.[2] Over and over, the message to the child of the alienating behavior is, "Believe me and choose me, or you'll lose my love; but in believing me, you'll have to reject your other parent." The child loses no matter what and ultimately doesn't know what is true.

But why psychologically abuse your own child? Parents manipulate their children for many reasons: animosity toward their former spouse, jealousy, or they may have a personality disorder that distorts their objectivity. Sometimes a biological parent starts alienating because their new spouse, the stepparent, wants to build a relationship with the kids. They surmise that pushing the biological parent in the other home out of the picture will help make their new stepfamily successful. Most often, parents manipulate children and engage in alienation out of revenge. Maybe they blame the other parent for the divorce or are embittered about the consequences of the divorce. Somehow, making the other parent pay seems to be the right response—and what better way to hurt a parent than by using their child against them?

A full and complete exploration of parental alienation is beyond the scope of this book. But let us say clearly here that this is not authentic rejection by the children. They are being manipulated. They are as much victims of the alienation as the alienated parent.

This important distinction reveals one way to combat alienation. Directly confront untruth being told to the child and empathize with the child's confusion that you know is going on under the surface. "I'm sorry you are being told I don't love you. I know you feel my love inside. It's confusing, I know. And I can see that you're caught in the middle, like you can't win for losing. I'm so sorry." Going deep into their heart to connect with the truth they experience is one way to cut through the lies.

If alienated already, applying the love language wisdom learned throughout this book is a good first strategy. You can try speaking their primary love language. But if that effort gets blocked (perhaps even by the child who is under the spell of their parent's manipulation), speak a secondary love language that is less intimate and, therefore, more likely to get through. For example, one dad found himself unable to give his daughter physical hugs or touch because she wouldn't even see him. He could, however, send her messages via text that expressed his heart and offered her words of affirmation. She didn't acknowledge the texts or reply for an extended period of time, and he didn't even know if she was receiving them. But she was. Eventually, when she began questioning what her mother had been saying, her father's persistent text messages and encouraging words landed on her heart and opened the way for reconciliation.

One final word: if you find yourself fighting alienation, reach out for resources and counsel.[3] Most co-parenting material is inadequate to address your circumstances, so find resources specifically on that subject and be sure to document everything that is going on because you may have to involve the court system. This can be a long and difficult road, but remember, what looks like rejection from a child may not be.

THE PATH THROUGH REJECTION: FAITHFUL LOVE

Sometimes only one of the above factors is contributing to rejection of a blended family member; other times, many of them are. Either way, what is needed in the face of rejection is the same: a long tenacious love that proves itself over time.

Contrary to popular belief, love is not all you need. You need tenacious love. Every intimate relationship needs love *and* faithfulness (or trustworthiness) coupled together. At best, love with-

Love without faithfulness leads to doubt and insecurity.

out faithfulness, even separate and apart from preexisting rejection, leads to doubt and insecurity. At worse, it causes deep hurt, adding more cause for rejection and a fracturing of the relationship.

An unreliable and uninvolved parent, despite telling their kids they love them, likely has children who question their worth, doubt whether they are loveable, and strive endlessly to be good enough in order to pull the parent back into their life. A spouse who commits infidelity traumatizes the trust between partners, causes hurt that can last for years, and may find themselves kicked out of their spouse's heart and the house.

And then there are situations where an obvious lack of faithfulness sabotages mutual love. A single dad who was dating a single mom shared the following. "We both love each other," he said. "I feel more loved by her than anyone ever." Then he explained his predicament. He and his girlfriend had been talking about engagement, but she was worried how a wedding and family merger would affect her four children. She suggested they marry but not tell the kids. According to her plan, they would continue to live in separate houses and make it appear to the kids and extended family that they were still dating. To have sex, they would wait for occasions when their kids were at their other parent's homes.

Would you sign on for this kind of arrangement? Does this sound like faithfulness to you? Would this arrangement foster emotional safety in their marriage, let alone in the family? We assure you, it will not. It doesn't matter how much they love each other, this lack of commitment will short-circuit their family experience in many ways.

Now, that's an extreme example. But it makes the point: love and faithfulness are critical to growing and sustaining healthy relationships. Rejection requires faithfulness in order to overcome what is behind the rejection.

Faithfulness and the love languages

In most relationships, especially romantic ones, love usually develops first, then trust, which deepens your experience of love. However, when facing rejection, the process is different. In order to first build trust, which can then open the door to love, stepparents have to be stubbornly persistent to show themselves faithful, even if a child or family member does not love you.

Consider this example. Strategically loving a rejecting child whose primary love language is Physical Touch with a fist bump for an extended period, while avoiding bear hugs because you know it makes them uncomfortable, is stubborn faithfulness that has a chance of becoming mutual love. In the face of their opposition, your continuing to love sends a powerful message that ultimately is hard to deny.

Likewise, being willing to repeatedly engage an adult child in surface-level dialogue around things that mean little to you, speaks the Quality Time language of their heart without forcing them to reveal too much about themselves. Of course, the hope is that pacing with them over time eventually opens their heart and decreases rejecting behavior.

How Can You Remain Faithful? Some Helpful Ideas

For most, overcoming rejection from a child or extended stepfamily member is simply a matter of persistent, stubborn love.

Wearing them down with faithful love is a pretty good strategy. The problem is, being faithful to love in the face of rejection is not simple to live out. Rejection hurts and is discouraging. What is needed is the resolve to keep going—and a few helpful tools.

Build your personal resolve. This in part is raw determination; there is much to be said for not giving up. But another part of resolve is not caring too much about winning the person's heart. That sounds counterintuitive, we know, so let us explain. Making the other's affection the object of your resolve gives them far too much power over your personal well-being and chips away at that resolve.

Instead, your resolve to remain faithful must be found "above and within." Find your sense of worth and identity in a relationship with the Divine, so you can separate who you really are from who the rejecting person implies you are. This will help you unhook from their definition of you. Finding significance from above and definition from within will fuel your resolve to continue knocking on the door of their heart without letting their resistance destroy you.

Releasing unmet expectations can also boost your resolve. One stepmom said she had to learn to let go of her expectations and hopes that her husband's daughter would appreciate what she does and who she is. Initially she was motivated to speak her stepdaughter's love language in order to "become her mom." In order to keep her resolve, she had to shift her motivation to "because it is the right thing to do for her in spite of her attitude toward me." She also focused on her husband. "If nothing else, it is loving toward my husband to continue speaking his daughter's love language."

Gently speak their love language. As the stepmom we just mentioned discovered, there's a difference between communicating love with the full expectation that the gesture or action will be reciprocated and gently communicating love with no expectation of anything in return. Offering a word of affirmation without the expectation of a "Thank you" or repeatedly going out of your way to perform an act of service when you know it won't be reciprocated communicates a stubborn, faithful love. And it does more than that.

Shaunti Feldhahn's research, reported in her book *The Kindness Challenge*, suggests that in addition to softening the heart of the recipient, setting your mind on kindly serving someone helps you to think more highly of the person to whom you are being kind.[4] It softens you and, hopefully, them. Why is it helpful for your heart to be softened when you're already motivated to build a relationship with them? Because it adds maturity to your motivation. You're more likely to have compassion for what's behind their rejection, and therefore, more able to depersonalize their actions and remain long-suffering. You're more insightful about their journey and what level of connection with you they can tolerate at this time. And you're more likely to notice positive changes in their attitude toward you.

By the way, if kindness helps you think more highly of the person you're being kind to, the opposite is also true. Thinking critically about someone makes you look for

> Thinking critically about someone makes you look for and notice more negatives about them.

and notice more negatives about them, thereby deepening your dislike for them. This just escalates mutual negativity. Rather, try to reverse this cycle by showing kindness. Repeatedly speaking a love language they can tolerate will help you remain faithful in loving them and might eventually soften their heart.

Do what you can. One new stepmom shared that her teenage stepdaughter had not been to their house for visitation for months due to her busy senior-year schedule. It really was not anyone's fault that they didn't have much time together. Life just got in the way. Because her stepdaughter had taken the online love languages profile, the stepmom knew her love language was Gifts. So she bought her a Starbucks gift card and mailed it to her with a note. "It was a small gesture," the stepmom said, "but she texted and thanked me for it." This simple but tangible act of kindness communicated love and bridged the gap.

Hang on to what's good. Do you remember the stepdad we quoted at the beginning of the chapter? The one who said loving his stepson was like beating his head against the wall? He later shared a strategy that helped him stay faithful to pursue his stepson. "When you see the child responding positively, even if they don't know how to express it, it helps. It encourages us to keep moving forward." Right. Any glimmer of light, even a faint one, brings hope. But sometimes to find that glimmer of hope, you have to look very intently for it.

Years ago a mentor of mine (Ron) suggested that I start "an encouragement file." Rereading a note of appreciation can help when we're having a bad day. Having the file did more than pick me up on a cloudy day; it forced me to pay attention to the positive feedback that was happening around me. What I instantly learned is that I receive far more com-

> You need to notice
> —*really notice*—when
> something positive
> happens.

pliments and words of appreciation than I realized.

Rejection is a heavy weight. To counter it, you need to notice—*really notice*—when something positive happens. Start collecting in a file, on your phone, or in a keepsake box the moments that encourage your heart. You might discover that a few positive exchanges are taking place even now and that all is not lost. Hang on to what's good.

Partner with your spouse. One stepmom with an adult stepdaughter was excluded from family birthdays, holidays, and activities of the grandkids. "She invites my husband," she said, "but not me. Should my husband attend those things without me? If he goes I'm worried it will discourage her from ever including me, but if he doesn't go out of respect for me, I'm concerned it will make things worse and he will grow to resent me." This is an example of competing attachments; both she and her husband are in a tough spot.

Though it feels like an either/or situation, they should utilize a both/and solution. That is, the father can choose both his wife and his adult daughter by initially compartmentalizing the relationships with the hope that they can merge them eventually. For example, since the husband (dad) is the "gateway" to the wife (stepmom) being included, we would suggest that he spend *some* time with his daughter and grandchildren without the stepmom, but then strategically include her in activities when everyone is present and holidays. We repeat: this is an initial "slow cooker" strategy meant to respect the daughter's pace and whatever is behind the rejection. But sooner or later, Dad may have to say to his daughter, "I know this is hard for you. But I need you to make space for her in our family life; meet her in the middle. You don't have to do it for her. If nothing else, please be decent to her out of your love for me."

Remember to say "thank you"

Rejection can be very defeating. Understanding what is behind the behavior and the power of faithful love to overcome it are important keys to not giving in to defeat.

In addition, it really helps when a spouse or other member of the family comes to the aid of a rejected stepparent or family member. Love and support throughout a desert experience encourages us to keep going. On a regular basis, speak the rejected person's primary love language and tell/show them how grateful you are for them and how sorry you are that they are experiencing rejection from someone else in the family. Empathy and a show of love from someone who sees the pain they are experiencing can help to sustain them while they hope for an open door.

YOUR TURN

Take inventory of who is feeling rejected in your family and who is rejecting them. Write down why you believe the rejection is taking place and what might be done about it. If it's someone else who is experiencing the rejection, go to them and express your empathy and love. If it's you that is dealing with rejection, identify someone you can go to for help or encouragement. Talk through the tools shared in this chapter and together decide what is your next step.

Encouragement for the Journey Ahead

"The one love language I tried didn't work. Or maybe
I wasn't doing it right . . . or they didn't want to receive it,
I'm not sure which."

"At times our blended family has been so confusing.
But I have had many years to figure out the love languages and
personalities of our kids. They are unique and add something
wonderful to our family. I'm thankful for their strengths and
weaknesses because otherwise I would have missed out on the joy
and blessing they bring to my life."

WHAT'S THE KEY DIFFERENCE between the two statements above? Time.

The first is from a frustrated stepparent who is feeling uncertain early in their family journey. The second, from a stepparent who has learned over time what works, what doesn't, and how to appreciate the uniqueness of each child. Extended time in the journey has brought the family together. This stepparent now sees their family as a beautiful mosaic.

Be encouraged in your journey to build love together and find a good blend. It's quite likely that the second stepparent quoted above shared the same sentiment as the first at some point in their journey. Stepfamily living can be challenging and confusing, especially in the early going. As one parent put it, "Everything in a blended family feels odd at times." But for many, great rewards follow that season of confusion. If you are reaping those rewards today, celebrate, and encourage someone else. If you are still confused or frustrated, don't give up on the process. Keep loving, keep that slow merging process going.

In the beginning, Elisha wasn't comfortable applying the love languages to her stepchildren and didn't know how to be a stepparent. She and her husband, Terry struggled to connect with one another's teenage kids. They first got intentional about *the blend* in their home by taking the online love language profile. Elisha saw the results and things began to make sense to her. She realized that her previous attempts to connect with her stepchildren missed their heart, and she redirected her efforts to scheduling quality time with her older stepchild and giving gifts to the younger one.

She also figured out that activities she scheduled that were centered around her interests weren't appealing to them; nor were they motivated at that point in time to speak her love language. Letting go of that expectation eased her disappointment and empowered her to keep loving with intentionality.

At the same time, Terry insightfully determined to move very slowly with his stepdaughter who had a good relationship with both her biological father and her first stepfather. Terry told her he valued those relationships for her and let her know he just wanted to find his place in her life without impinging on her relationship with them. That started the slow simmering process for the two of them. She respected his posture and over time figured out where to put him in her heart.

ADULT STEPKIDS LOOK BACK

Wouldn't it be great if you could apply love language principles to the blended family with confidence that it would pay off? What if you knew which behaviors had the most impact so you could target your efforts even more?

It's always encouraging to hear success stories from parents, but success stories can be even more convincing when you hear them from young adult children who have some life perspective. Still others want research to back up the advice. One study we'd like to share with you brought these two data points together.

Building on previous research, researchers asked adult step-children with a positive relationship with their stepparent to look back over time and examine what moved their relationship toward positivity and health.[1] Instead of asking adults or children in the throes of merging their families what made them happy or felt good, they asked young adult children who had the advantage of hindsight and years in their blended family. Keep in mind they didn't plant ideas in the participants' minds, for example, about "quality time," and thereby bias their responses. The researchers simply asked them what made a difference, then categorized the responses and analyzed them. Much of what they learned about the behaviors that turn stepchild-stepparent relationships in the right direction (what they called "turning points") reflects the principles taught in this book. We hope the following insight from that study encourages you to continue loving with intentionality, even when you don't see an immediate benefit.

Beyond expectations

Though the researchers didn't study the five love languages per se, some of the behaviors they documented as being most significant echo our discussion for blended families in this book almost exactly. What the researchers called "prosocial actions" included behaviors like giving gifts (Gifts), engaging in acts of kindness (Acts of Service), and communicating positive messages to the child (Words of Affirmation). When stepparents repeatedly engaged in these actions, adult stepchildren reported that ultimately they were transformative for the relationship, especially when stepparents went above and beyond what the child expected or anticipated from them.

As we have suggested throughout this book, the full impact of these behaviors won't necessarily be immediate. It may take years before either of you can look back and say that any given action was a "turning point" in your relationship. But ultimately, such steps can result in great gains for your family.

The study found that the element of surprise made a difference. When the stepparent did something unexpected for the child, she or he felt loved, cared for, supported.[2] For example, one specific positive turning point uncovered in the research occurred when a stepparent talked about or to the child as if they were "my own" (powerful Words of Affirmation). It showed the child their worth to the stepparent. Over time, positive emotional experiences like this can relax the heart of the recipient, in this case a child, and open them to deeper trust and connection.

It is worth noting that children did not always immediately relate to this language, nor did they reciprocate and speak of their stepparent as "their own." Nevertheless, the research suggests they internalized the stepparent's desire for them, which seems eventually to have softened and opened their heart.

What about Physical Touch? We think appropriate touch, gently given over time, can have the same effect. Don't get discouraged if referring to a child as your own doesn't produce immediate results in how they respond to you. Just stay calm and stay the course. Remember, it is faithful love over time that merges hearts and grows a family.

Quality Time

Spending Quality Time with someone communicates that you value them and gives you a chance to build memories together that help give definition and shape to your relationship. This was supported by the research. Examples of "positive Quality Time turning points" included having fun together in a family group or one-on-one activity, making meals together, traveling, and engaging in side by side mentoring moments (like teaching a child to drive). Helpful conversations about life and relationships sometimes made a child feel supported, especially when they included words of encouragement from the stepparent. Even the first blended family vacation resulted in a 30 percent increase in positivity with the stepparent.[3]

But here's an important insight. The researchers discovered that quality time rarely occurred early in the family journey because of conflict, which is common during that phase. Who wants to spend intimate time with someone you don't like or at least, don't know what to do with? Quality Time, especially meaningful one-on-one time, becomes more likely as children age into late adolescence or adulthood when the relationship has had time to solidify and become more positive in general. Do you remember in chapter 3 when we suggested that some love languages and dialects are more intimate than others and you have to move into them slowly? This research insight supports what we were talking about. You cannot force intimate time on a child; it has to come gradually as a result of your slow blending.

Let's say it another way. If *your* love language is Quality Time, sacrifice the more intense dialect of one-on-one time and look for group family activities or limited one-on-one time until the relationship is strong enough to enjoy more prolonged, focused time together. Grow into it with wisdom.

Considered together, Quality Time and what the researchers called "prosocial actions" (including what we refer to as Gifts, Acts of Service, Words of Affirmation) were the top two positive turning point responses (out of thirteen). They accounted for one-third of the positive change moments reported by now adult stepchildren in their stepparent relationship.[4] Clearly, their positive effect is significant. This should be encouraging.

The impact was especially true when stepchildren felt uncertain about their relationship with their stepparent. That is, when they felt distant from the stepparent, but the stepparent went out of their way to surprise them with a gift or stand up for them in a social setting, the action made a significant difference in the relationship. Here's the takeaway for stepparents: leading with love, even when uncertain about the relationship or it seems out of balance, has the power of being a turning point for good.

If children are with you part-time and it's hard to find a rhythm for expressing love, strive to make the most of the time you do have and go all out on holidays and special family days. Building memories and rituals that say "We are family" can help.

The study identified many other less common and less impactful, though still important, turning points that contributed positive changes for the relationship such as moving into a new house, developing holiday traditions that held meaning for the family, and surviving a crisis together. Even stepparent-stepchild conflict was found to be helpful when resolved (that is, when reconciliation occurred after a conflict).[5] But actions that clearly expressed love to the child were the highest reported and over time seemed to hold the most positive impact.

We should mention that not all well-intended behaviors produced a positive change in the relationship. Some occurrences had a neutral impact, according to the adult stepchildren, while a very small percentage actually had a negative impact. The reminder here is that not every effort on your part will bring about positive change. The vast majority will—*eventually*. A few will not. Love anyway, because over time you build undeniable evidence of your heart and desire for connection and the cumulative positive impact far outweighs everything else.

KEY TAKEAWAYS

Let us summarize the implications of this research for your family as it relates to the five love languages.

- Loving extravagantly and faithfully over time with behaviors like Gift Giving, Words of Affirmation, Acts of Service, Physical Touch, and sharing Quality Time, ultimately moves steprelationships in a positive direction. These behaviors require little time, skill, money, or effort, but have significant impact.

- Unexpected, surprising actions speak loudly and are hard to miss.
- Quality Time is tougher to orchestrate early on because the tension surrounding family integration makes it uncomfortable. Be measured in the beginning of your family journey (pace with the kids) and increase your quality time efforts as relationships prove ready for it.
- The positive impact of speaking someone's love language is not usually felt immediately but becomes more evident over time. Even after experiencing a positive shift in their feelings toward a stepparent, a child may not reciprocate their love until sometime later.
- Stepparents should enter the parental role of disciplinarian slowly and cautiously. As we discussed in chapter 5, focus first on building friendship, trust, and love, then move into boundary setting and setting rules.
- Negative conflict, when processed and resolved and the relationship reconciled, can become a positive turning point for stepparents and stepchildren. It builds resilience and a perceived sense of value to the other.
- Taken as a whole, everything from simple, everyday behaviors to "above and beyond" actions powerfully communicate authentic love to a child and have strength to improve the quality of the relationship.

This last takeaway is worth repeating. Many couples report feeling powerless to bring their family together or improve a stressful stepfamily relationship. Faithful love is your power; it has the muscle you need to turn things in a better direction.

BLENDING OF THE SANDS

Many people are familiar with the unity candle ceremony at weddings. Many blended family weddings today incorporate a ceremony called "Blending of the Sands" that has similar symbolic meaning. Glass vases holding different colored sands represent the various adults and children the marriage will merge. The couple first symbolically pours some sand from their individual vase into a larger "family" vase. Then each child is invited to do the same. The beautiful blend of sand makes a mosaic that can be taken home and displayed as a lasting visual representation of the coming together of the family.

But does the mosaic suggest that the family has at that point found unity?

A wedding is important to marriage because it marks the end of something and the beginning of something. A wedding marks the end or culmination of a process in which two people meet, fall in love, agree to a shared vision for life, and choose to commit themselves to one another "so long as we both shall live." A wedding marks the beginning of those two people living out their vows. New boundaries are drawn, new loyalties declared, and new allegiance determined. Friends and family, even the government, are put on notice. Vows have been taken, a new life begun, and everyone must adapt accordingly. From this moment on, things are different.

The rituals of a wedding are meant to help drive this point home (for both the couple, their children, if they have them, and all witnesses). Giving wedding rings is a good example. The pastor usually explains the symbolism. "A ring is a circle. It has no beginning or end; it is continuous. And so, your covenant promises to one another will not end." Similarly, the unity candle ceremony invites couples to take their individual candle and light a larger, unifying candle as a symbol of their desire toward oneness. *And the two shall become one.*

Rituals are serious business. But no one who witnesses the couple light the candle assumes they've obtained spiritual, emotional, physical, and intellectual oneness. We just recognize that lighting the candle starts a process that calls them to it.

Strive for it, is the message of the unity candle ceremony. *Orient your life around finding oneness. Die to yourself and put off selfishness; now you're living for the "us-ness" of your marriage,* is the call of the ritual. *There's a ring on your finger, live like it.*

In effect, the ritual drives a stake in the ground, draws a line in the sand, and points to a future that will be different because of what just happened. But it doesn't assume for one minute that the oneness goal has been obtained.

Likewise, blended families start a journey on the wedding day that is not culminated until much later. Having a Blending of the Sands ceremony in your wedding does not mean you have actually obtained "familyness." It does not culminate *the blend,* it begins the process. A line has been drawn, there is no going back, "We are now building love together" is the declaration made by the parents, but now they must figure out how to practically work with each family member to define what that means and move toward it.

During a wedding, in the Blending of the Sands ceremony children and adults alike pour most, if not all, of their personal sand into the large family vase. In real life, one child pours in half and saves half for the other home they live in. A second child pours in most of themselves, but with mixed emotions, then tries to take some back, while yet a third child in protest pinches a few grains of sand with their fingers and flicks them toward the family vase. Motivations to love vary. Definitions of what loving people will look like differ. The need of children for their parents not to put so much of themselves in the vase often competes with the desire of the parents to pour in all of themselves.

But they have started the process of building love together.

A Blending of the Sands ceremony immediately produces a beautiful sand art montage. In real life, blended families often immediately look irregular, disjointed, and as one parent said, "odd." During *the blend,* the grit of the sand coursing against other sands is abrasive. With time, however, the various sands combine and grow comfortable with each other, add more of themselves, and form a stunning mosaic of colors and shapes.

If you were to ask that family mosaic, "How did you get to be this beautiful?" it may be able to identify some turning points. Other factors remain a mystery. But the narrative that is likely to tie it all together is love—intentional, purposeful, sacrificial, faithful love.

YOUR TURN

Identify and discuss any turning points that have helped your family already. Then share specific actions this chapter is prompting you to take in the future. Finally, describe your family mosaic as of today. Where are you in the process of blending your sands and how can you stay encouraged for the journey ahead?

Epilogue

CO-AUTHORING A BOOK with Ron Deal has been a delightful journey. For over twenty-five years he has worked intimately with stepfamilies, helping them to become blended families. For over twenty-five years, I have been sharing the message of the five love languages. I have seen this simple concept change thousands of marriages, and greatly enhance parent-child relationships. I believe that discovering the primary love language of another person and speaking it consistently, while sprinkling in the other four languages, is the road to good relationships.

Through the years, so many couples that are in a second or third marriage have asked me, "How do the love languages work in a blended family?" This book is my answer to that question. Ron's years of experience and his willingness to share his insights and real-life illustrations have made the book extremely practical.

As you have read the book, I think you have found your own thoughts and emotions expressed in the words of others. Dreams of love and unity dance in the minds and hearts of couples that are establishing a blended family. The pain and hurt of the past, caused by the dissolution of a relationship or the death of a spouse, still linger in the heart, but you see a new day ahead; a day you have longed for and dreamed about, and often prayed for.

Now you have once again found love and trust in another. You eagerly anticipate joining your lives together to build the marriage you have always longed for: a loving, caring, supportive relationship that will help both of you reach your potential for good in the world. However, you soon discover that your world is larger than the two of you. If he has children, you are now a stepmom. If she has children, you are now a stepdad. If your former spouses are still alive, you will likely share the children. If your spouse died you have not forgotten him/her, nor have your children. Your family just got bigger and more complex.

What we have sought to share is a road map that leads to a truly blended family. Not all blended families will look the same. Some will find real connectedness; genuine love will flow between family members. Others will encounter roadblocks that will take them on a detour route. However, persistent expressions of love in the right language are the most effective way to get back on the road to becoming a truly blended family.

It is our hope that if you find this book helpful, you will share it with your friends who are on a similar journey. They too want what you want: a loving, supportive family in which each family member is seeking to encourage and help the other. It is our desire that thousands of couples will see their dreams come true as they apply the principles in this book.

—Gary Chapman

Acknowledgments

I (GARY) HAVE GREATLY admired Ron Deal's ministry to blended families through the years. It is my privilege to join him in this book on how the love languages relate to blended families.

Deepest thanks to my wife, Karolyn, who edited the manuscript before we submitted it to the publisher. Thanks also to Anita Hall, my administrative assistant, who helped greatly in preparing the manuscript. And thank you to the wonderful team at Northfield Publishing: John Hinkley, Betsey Newenhuyse, and all those involved in every phase of the process.

I (RON) AM SO APPRECIATIVE to Gary Chapman for his life of service to others. He has made my marriage better, he's made me a better dad, and his body of work has helped me help others with their relationships. Collaborating with him on this project has been an honor.

My thanks to John Hinkley and the Northfield Publishing team for entertaining my idea and then cheering on the project from the beginning. Special thanks to assistants Anita Hall and Shannon Simmons, and Karolyn Chapman (unofficial editor) and Betsey Newenhuyse (official editor) for making this book readable and clear. I can't thank my agent Chip MacGregor enough; he is a trusted friend and I'm very grateful for his guidance.

And to my family: I am a blessed man, with three sons I love more than life and who love me right back, warts and all. And to Nan: Thank you for building a lifetime of love with me. I.L.Y.M.T.M.L.

Notes

Introduction
1. Online survey conducted by Ron Deal and Smart Stepfamilies, 2018.

Chapter 1: Blending Well, Loving Well
1. Not her real name. Throughout the book names and details of real people have been changed to protect individual and family privacy.
2. Patricia Papernow, *Becoming a Stepfamily: Patterns of Development in Remarried Families* (New York: Gardner Press, 1993), 387.
3. Ron L. Deal, *The Smart Stepfamily: Seven Steps to a Healthy Family*, revised and expanded ed. (Bloomington, MN: Bethany House Publishers, 2014), 93–98.
4. See Emily E. Wiemers et al., "Stepfamily Structure and Transfers between Generations in U.S. Families," paper presented at the 2015 annual meeting of the Population Association of America, San Diego, CA, July 2018, http://public.econ.duke.edu/~vjh3/working_papers/StepkinTransfers.pdf.
5. For a full discussion of the blended family divorce rate see Ron L. Deal, *The Smart Stepfamily*, revised and expanded ed. (Bloomington, MN: Bethany House Publishers, 2014), 101–102.

Chapter 2: Understanding the Languages of Love
1. The notion that relationships need both love and trustworthiness to foster identity (a sense of worth) and safety ("this relationship is reliable") comes from the work of good friend Terry Hargrave, PhD, found in his coauthored book *Restoration Therapy: Understanding and Guiding Healing in Marriage and Family Therapy* (New York: Routledge, 2011).
2. Parts of this section are adapted from Deborah Barr, Edward G. Shaw, and Gary Chapman, *Keeping Love Alive as Memories Fade: The 5 Love Languages and the Alzheimer's Journey* (Chicago: Northfield Publishing, 2016), 38–39.
3. A word we like to use that represents what is created when two people belong to and contribute to a cherished, permanent relationship.
4. Ancient texts like the Bible and modern theories of psychotherapy (see *Restoration Therapy* by Terry Hargrave) have long taught the importance of trustworthiness and keeping our promises. And even though we usually talk

about love as if it's enough for relationships, we all intuitively know a love you can't trust won't result in a safe, intimate relationship.

5. See Terry Hargrave's *Restoration Therapy* (New York: Routledge, 2011).

Chapter 3: When Loves Compete and Conflict

1. Adapted from Deborah Barr, Edward G. Shaw, and Gary Chapman, *Keeping Love Alive as Memories Fade: The 5 Love Languages and the Alzheimer's Journey* (Chicago: Northfield Publishing, 2016), 38–40.

2. Dawn O. Braithwaite et al., "'Feeling Warmth and Close to Her': Communication and Resilience Reflected in Turning Points in Positive Adult Stepchild–Stepparent Relationships," *Journal of Family Communication* 18, no. 2 (2018): 92–109, https://www.tandfonline.com/doi/full/10.1080/15267431.2017.141 5902

Chapter 4: Building Love Together in Your Marriage

1. Lauren Reitsema, *In Their Shoes: Helping Parents Better Understand and Connect with Children of Divorce* (Bloomington, MN: Bethany House, 2019).

2. Blended family financial matters are discussed at length in *The Smart Stepfamily Guide to Financial Planning: Money Management Before and After You Blend a Family* (Minneapolis: Bethany House, 2019) by Ron L. Deal, Greg S. Pettys, and David O. Edwards.

3. Adapted from Gary Chapman, *The 5 Love Languages: The Secret to Love That Lasts* (Chicago: Northfield Publishing, 2015), 37–118.

Chapter 5: Building Love Together in Stepparenting

1. Learn more about this "No-Threat Message" in *The Smart Stepmom* (Bloomington, MN: Bethany House Publishers, 2009) by Ron Deal and Laura Petherbridge; and in *The Smart Stepdad* (Bloomington, MN: Bethany House Publishers, 2011) by Ron Deal.

2. We recommend Gary's book *When Sorry Isn't Enough: Making Things Right with Those You Love* with Jennifer Thomas (Chicago: Northfield Publishing, 2013).

3. Adapted from *The 5 Love Languages of Children* by Gary Chapman and Ross Campbell (Chicago: Northfield Publishing, 2016), 113–16. Used with permission.

Chapter 6: Building Love Together in Sibling Relationships

1. Larry Bumpass, "Some Characteristics of Children's Second Families," *American Journal of Sociology* 90, no. 3 (November 1984): 608–23.

2. Susan L. Brown, Wendy D. Manning, and J. Bart Stykes, "Family Structure and Child Well-Being: Integrating Family Complexity," *Journal of Marriage and Family* 77, no. 1 (February 2015): 177–90. For a more complete discussion of the difficulties in counting half- and stepsibling relationships see Lawrence Ganong and Marilyn Coleman, *Stepfamily Relationships: Development, Dynamics, and Interventions*, 2nd ed. (New York: Springer, 2017), 191–92.

3. Ganoag and Coleman, *Stepfamily Relationships*, 202–204.

4. Ibid., 202.
5. Debra Mekos, E. Mavis Hetherington, and David Reiss, "Sibling Differences in Problem Behavior and Parental Treatment in Nondivorced and Remarried Families," *Child Development* 67, no. 5 (October 1996): 2148–165. As reported in Ganong and Coleman, *Stepfamily Relationships*, 202.
6. Ron L. Deal, *Daily Encouragement for the Smart Stepfamily* (Bloomington, MN: Bethany House Publisher, 2018), 209.
7. Ron L. Deal, *The Smart Stepfamily: Seven Steps to a Healthy Family* (Bloomington, MN: Bethany House Publishers, 1994), 277–85.
8. Ron L. Deal, "What Do We Do Now? When Stepsiblings Have Sex," Smart Stepfamilies, https://smartstepfamilies.com/view/stepsibling-romance.
9. I'm (Ron Deal) so grateful I heard my friend Bob Maday make this statement. I knew it was right—and profound—the moment I heard him say it.

Chapter 7: Building Love Together in Grandparenting

1. Maximiliane E. Szinovacz, "Grandparents Today: A Demographic Profile," *The Gerontologist* 38, no. 1 (1998): 37–52.
2. Kenneth W. Wachter, "Kinship Resources for the Elderly," *Philosophical Transactions of the Royal Society of London Biological Sciences* 352, no. 1363 (December 1997): 1811–817. The ratio for Americans will be one stepgrandchild for every 1.7 biological grandchild.
3. Lauren Reitsema, *In Their Shoes: Helping Parents Better Understand and Connect with Children of Divorce* (Bloomington, MN: Bethany House Publishers, 2019).
4. Lawrence Ganong and Marilyn Coleman, *Stepfamily Relationships: Development, Dynamics, and Intervention*, 2nd ed. (New York: Springer, 2017), 214–26.
5. Ibid., 222.

Chapter 8: Building Love Together in the Face of Rejection

1. Gary's book with Jennifer Thomas entitled *When Sorry Isn't Enough: Making Things Right with Those You Love* (Chicago: Northfield Publishing, 2013) might help.
2. As heard on the podcast *FamilyLife Blended with Ron Deal* in an episode entitled "Challenging Co-Parent Situations and Parent Alienation," April 29, 2019, familylife.com/podcast/familylife-blended-podcast/6-challenging-co-parent-situations-and-parent-alienation/. Listen to all of Ron's podcasts here: https://www.familylife.com/podcast/familylife-blended-podcast/.
3. Visit Parental Alienation Awareness Organization USA at https://www.paaousa.org/. One recommended book is *Divorce Poison: How to Protect Your Family from Bad-mouthing and Brainwashing*, new and updated ed. (New York: HarperCollins, 2010) by Dr. Richard A. Warshak.
4. Shaunti Feldhahn, *The Kindness Challenge: Thirty Days to Improve Any Relationship* (Colorado Springs, CO: WaterBrook, 2016).

Chapter 9: Encouragement for the Journey Ahead

1. Dawn O. Braithwaite et al., "'Feeling Warmth and Close to Her': Communication and Resilience Reflected in Turning Points in Positive Adult Stepchild–Stepparent Relationships," *Journal of Family Communication* 18, no. 2 (January 2018): 92–109, https://www.tandfonline.com/doi/full/10.1080/15267431.2017.1415902

2. Ibid., 97–98.

3. Ibid., 98–99.

4. Braithwaite et al. did not ask about aspects of Physical Touch nor did respondents spontaneously offer observations that would fall into this category.

5. Ibid., 99–100. Though "reconciliation/problem solving" was less common as a reported turning point, it had a positive effect. Taking the time to resolve conflict moves hearts toward emotional safety.

RENOVATE YOUR RELATIONAL SPACE

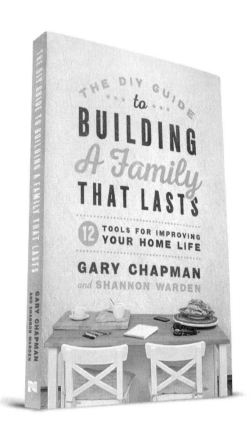

STRENGTHENING MILLIONS OF RELATIONSHIPS— ONE LANGUAGE AT A TIME

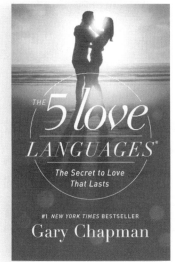

978-0-8024-1270-6

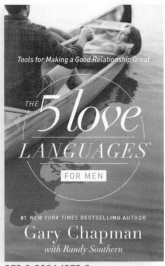

978-0-8024-1272-0

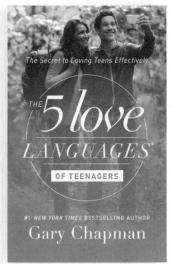

978-0-8024-1284-3

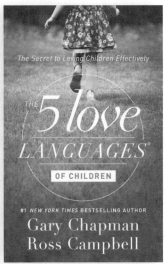

978-0-8024-1285-0

also available as eBooks and audiobooks